BOOK OF
INSULTS
AND
IRREVERENT
QUOTATIONS

BOOK OF INSULTS AND IRREVERENT QUOTATIONS

DONALD D. HOOK
and
LOTHAR KAHN

Jonathan David Publishers, Inc.
Middle Village, NY 11379

BOOK OF INSULTS
AND
IRREVERENT QUOTATIONS
by
Donald D. Hook and Lothar Kahn

Copyright © 1980

by
JONATHAN DAVID PUBLISHERS, INC.
68-22 ELIOT AVENUE
MIDDLE VILLAGE, NEW YORK 11379

Library of Congress Cataloging in Publication Data
Main entry under title:

Book of insults and irreverent quotations.

1. Invective. 2. Quotations, English. I. Hook,
Donald D., 1928-   II. Kahn, Lothar. III. Title.
PN6231.I65B64   081   80-13895
ISBN 0-8246-0250-1

Printed in the United States of America

Table of Contents

A Note About the Style

The name of the person who is the subject of the insult is set in capital letters.

The name that appears under each quotation is that of the person to whom the statement is ascribed.

Every effort was made to ascertain the profession and/or nationality of every insulter quoted. Regrettably, there are several instances where this information could not be determined.

····
Preface

This book is not meant to insult, to teach the art of insulting, or to make a cult of the insult. Even without books on insults, far too many individuals complain, with or without justification, about being the targets of barbs, digs, aspersions, affronts, and indignities. We are, after all, not living in an age of spiritual harmony.

Our intention in presenting this collection of insults and irreverent quotations is, perhaps primarily, to provide entertainment. At the same time, however, we hope to show how, in other equally restless times, notables have let off steam or simply amused themselves by taking a crack at people who had hurt or slighted them, whom they disliked, whom they regarded as hostile.

The insults presented here range from the mild—i.e., the epigrammatic—to the downright rude and ugly, but the bulk contains a healthy dose of humor and exaggeration. Like all good humor and most effective affronts, many of the statements have a serious base. Some of the insults and irreverent comments could be shrugged off by the insultee with a forebearing look and a vow to respond in kind, while others, sharper and more vicious, may have hit a vulnerable spot and scored more sharply. This latter type of insult has become rare in modern times as libel laws and other protective measures have prompted greater care and caution. As a result, the blatant insult of yesteryear has often become mere innuendo, equally aggressive but more subtle, yet perhaps lacking somewhat in forthrightness and honesty.

The public has always demonstrated a strong liking for remarks both brash and clever. Newspapers and magazines use them as fillers, and comedians and actors employ them cleverly to "roast" fellow celebrities on television comedy hours. People still enjoy a hearty laugh at the weaknesses of others.

An old biblical admonition cautions: "When your enemy stumbles, do not rejoice." Nonetheless, this very tendency has remained a weakness of humankind: we do get our biggest kicks at the expense of others. Since human nature doesn't seem to change, let's at least learn to enjoy the faults and failures we observe in our fellowman without malice. This book, it is our hope, will provide many hearty laughs that are enjoyed without malice.

Chapter One

. . . .

U.S. PRESIDENTS

Today an American presidential campaign begins shortly after the last one has ended. It intensifies steadily until a year before the next election, when all party organs, public relations firms, newspapers, and TV commentators and pollsters address themselves almost exclusively to the emerging candidates. The tons of pages printed and millions of words spoken in the course of a campaign include insults by the thousand.

A century ago, when campaigns were short and the verbiage less, greater care was expended on the criticism of opponents. The insults were fewer, although perhaps more pungent, but the circus atmosphere was similar, as was the desire to demolish the "wrong" candidate with one devastating label or catchy phrase.

Of course, not all insults came from campaign oratory. The personalities and images of candidates, whether real or imagined, have always impressed themselves on the public, and opponents have tried to make political capital of them. The aristocratic bearing of the Adamses of Boston, the "immoralities" of Jefferson, the bravado of Theodore Roosevelt, the moral piety and self-righteousness of Woodrow Wilson, the silences of Calvin Coolidge—all were the subject of satire and insult. Presidents as hated and loved as Abraham Lincoln and Franklin D. Roosevelt found themselves the target of innumerable barbs.

The moment a politician enters the presidential political ring he had better raise his gloves in vigorous defense and be prepared to deal some blows of his own. Politics is not for the thin-skinned. The quotations in this chapter are testimony to that.

ADAMS, JOHN
1735-1826, second U.S. president

Ali Baba among his Forty Thieves is no more deserving of sympathy than John Adams shut up within the seclusion of his Cabinet room with his official family of secret enemies.
—Claude G. Bowers, author

[He is an] eccentric, [lacks] sound judgment, [and possesses] vanity without bounds [and] a jealousy capable of discoloring every object.
—Alexander Hamilton, first secretary of the U.S. Treasury

He can't dance, drink, game, flatter, promise, dress, swear with the gentlemen, and small talk and flirt with the ladies —in short, he has none of the essential arts or ornaments which make up a courtier—there are thousands who with a tenth part of his understanding, and without a spark of his honesty, would distance him infinitely in any court in Europe.

—Jonathan Sewall, in Page Smith's
John Adams 1784-1826

It has been the political career of this man to begin with hypocrisy, proceed with arrogance, and finish with contempt.

—Tom Paine, political theorist

He is distrustful, obstinate, excessively vain, and takes no counsel from anyone.

—Thomas Jefferson, U.S. president

ADAMS, JOHN QUINCY
1767-1848, sixth U.S. president

Of all the men, whom it was ever my lot to accost and to waste civilities upon, [he] was the most doggedly and systematically repulsive. With a vinegar aspect, cotton in his leathern ears, and hatred of England in his heart, he sat in the frivolous assemblies of Petersburg like a bull-dog among spaniels; and many were the times that I drew monosyllables and grim smiles from him and tried in vain to mitigate his venom.

—W.H. Lyttleton, English politician
and governor of North Carolina

When they talk about his old age and venerableness and nearness to the grave, he knows better. He is like one of those old cardinals, who as quick as he is chosen Pope, throws away his crutches and his crookedness, and is straight as a boy. He is an old roué, who cannot live on slops, but must have sulphuric acid in his tea.

—Ralph Waldo Emerson,
poet and essayist

Quiet is not his sphere. And when a legitimate scene of action does not present itself, it is much to be feared that he will embrace an illegitimate one.

—Charles Francis Adams, in Marie B.
Hecht's *John Quincy Adams, A Personal History of an Independent Man*

Well has he been called "The Massachusetts Madman." He boasts that he places all his glory in independence. If independence is synonymous with obstinacy, he is the most independent statesman living.

—Anonymous

John Quincy Adams was a short, stout, bald, brilliant and puritanical twig off a short, stout, bald, brilliant, and puritanical tree. Little wonder, then, that he took the same view of the office of President as had his father.

—Alfred Steinberg, author

I am a man of reserved, cold and forbidding manners.

—On himself

ARTHUR, CHESTER ALAN
1830-1886, twenty-first U.S. president

A non entity with side whiskers.

—attributed to Woodrow Wilson,
U.S. president

... Chester A. Arthur, who became honest after becoming president.

—Richard Armour, author

First in ability on the list of second-rate men.

—Anonymous

Chet Arthur, President of the U.S.! Good God!

—a New York political associate

BUCHANAN, JAMES
1791-1868, fifteenth U.S. president

Yankee Doodle keep it up,
  It's all as clear as figgers,
Buchanan is the candidate
  To raise the price of niggers.

—pro-Frémont campaign song

There is no such person running as James Buchanan. He is dead of lockjaw. Nothing remains but a platform and a bloated mass of political putridity.

—Thaddeus Stevens, U.S. congressman

The Constitution provides for every accidental contingency in the Executive—except a vacancy in the mind of the President.

—John Sherman, U.S. senator
from Ohio

By half measures, evasions and stealthy approaches, by all the arts of weakness, he had gained the Presidency at just the moment when a man of all but superhuman vision and strength was needed.

—Allan Nevins, historian

CARTER, JAMES EARL

1924-   , thirty-ninth U.S. president

I was in Washington recently, and Jimmy was buying four new suits. As tight as Jimmy is, he wouldn't be buying new suits if he wasn't going to run again.

—Billy Carter, brother
of the president

They say Carter is the first businessman ever to sit in the White House. But why did they have to send us a small businessman.

—George Meany, president
of AFL-CIO

I once called Carter a "chicken-fried McGovern," and I take that back because I've come to respect McGovern.

—Robert Dole, U.S. senator

CLEVELAND, (STEPHEN) GROVER

1837-1908, twenty-second and twenty-fourth U.S. president

To nominate Grover Cleveland would be to arch through a slaughter house into an open grave.

—Henry Watterson, journalist

Harrison is a wise man,
   Cleveland is a fool;
Harrison rides a white horse
   Cleveland rides a mule.

—Republican campaign jingle of 1892

We have been told that the mantle of Tilden has fallen upon Cleveland. The mantle of a giant upon the shoulders of a dwarf!

—William Bourke Cockran, U.S.
congressman, lawyer, politician,
and orator

He was not a cruel man, but he was dogmatic, obtuse, and insensitive.

—Richard Hofstadter, author

A man of force & stubborness with no breadth of view, no training in our history & traditions & essentially coarse fibred & self sufficient.

—Henry Cabot Lodge, U.S.
senator from Massachusetts

COOLIDGE, (JOHN) CALVIN
1872-1933, thirtieth U.S. president

When an excited man rushed up to Wilson Mizner and said, "Coolidge is dead," Mizner asked, "How do they know?"

—Alva Johnston, author; also attributed
to Dorothy Parker, columnist

I think the American people want a solemn ass as President. And I think I'll go along with them.

—On himself

He slept more than any other President, whether by day or night, Nero fiddled, but Coolidge only snored. When the crash came at last and Hoover began to smoke and bubble, good Cal was safe in Northampton, and still in the hay.

—H.L. Mencken, author and critic

. . . this runty, aloof, little man, who quacks through his nose when he speaks.

—William Allen White, author

. . . one day I was at my doctor's. When I came in he was grinning with amusement and said, "Mrs. Longworth, the patient who has just left said something that I am sure will make you laugh. We were discussing the President, and he remarked, 'Though I yield to no one in my admiration for Mr. Coolidge, I do wish he did not look as if he had been weaned on a pickle.'" Of course I shouted with pleasure and told everyone, always carefully giving credit to the un-named originator, but in a very short time it was attributed to me.

—Alice Roosevelt Longworth, socialite

He was an economic fatalist with a God-given inertia. He knew nothing and refused to learn.

—William Allen White, journalist

EISENHOWER, DWIGHT DAVID
1890-1969, thirty-fourth U.S. president

Here we have at the top a cardiac case whose chief in-terest is in getting away from his job as often as possible for golf and bridge.

—I.F. Stone, commentator and publisher;
editor of *I.F. Stone's Weekly*

If I talk over the people's head, Ike must be talking under their feet.

—Adlai Stevenson, statesman

Golf is a fine release from the tensions of office, but we are a little tired of holding the bag.

—Adlai Stevenson

The Republicans have a "me too" candidate running on a "yes but" platform, advised by a "has-been" staff.

—Adlai Stevenson

As an intellectual, he bestowed upon the games of golf and bridge all the enthusiasm and perseverance that he withheld from books and ideas.

—Emmet John Hughes,
author and journalist

Golf had long symbolized the Eisenhower years—played by soft, boring men with ample waistlines who went around rich men's country-club courses in the company of wealthy businessmen and were tended by white-haired, dutiful Negroes.

—David Halberstam, author

I read a very interesting quote by Senator Kerr of Oklahoma. In summing up Ike, he said "Eisenhower is the only living unknown soldier." Even this is giving him all the best of it.

—Groucho Marx, comedian

I can think of nothing more boring, for the American public, than to have to sit in their living rooms for a whole half an hour looking at my face on their television screens.

—On himself

You know, once in a while I get to the point, with everybody staring at me, where I want to go back indoors and pull down the curtains.

—On himself

The trouble with Eisenhower is he's just a coward. He hasn't got any backbone at all.

—Harry Truman, U.S. president

FILLMORE, MILLARD
1800-1874, thirteenth U.S. president

A Vain and Handsome Mediocrity.

—Glyndon G. Van Deusen, author

FORD, GERALD RUDOLPH
1913-   , thirty-eighth U.S. president

I've never met him, but I used to spend time in Ohio, and they turn out Jerry Fords by the bale.

—Alice Roosevelt Longworth, socialite

Poor, dull Jerry.

—Betty Ford, wife of President Ford

I wish I'd married a plumber. At least he'd be home by 5 o'clock.

—Betty Ford

I can't possibly believe Jerry's a dumb-dumb. He couldn't possibly have been reelected from the district all these years.

—Betty Ford

Mediocre is a word in Grand Rapids often used to describe him, as though that would be the best kind of official to have.

—Peter Rand

Gerald Ford is one of the relatively few living Americans who not only admires Richrd Nixon but actually *likes* him.

—Larry L. King, writer

I cannot dislike him personally—he's cordial and gracious. But he's consistently wrong, and consistency is a virtue of small minds. He's never proposed a constructive solution to anything.

—Robert F. Drinan, U.S. Congressman

He doesn't have the intellect and magnificence of Adlai Stevenson, the flourish of John Kennedy, or the fire of Spiro Agnew—but he tends to be more believable and sincere than Richard Nixon.

—Michael Doyle

Jerry doesn't really have a 1st-class mind. But, then, neither did Eisenhower.

—Ford staff member

Ford isn't a bad man, but he's dumb-dumb. He shouldn't be dumb either. He went to school just like everybody else.

—The Reverend Duncan Littlfair

He has a slow mind, but he has backbone.

—Barber Conable, U.S. congressman

I'm a Ford, not a Lincoln. My addresses will never be as eloquent.

—On himself

I got the impression of a fellow with the mind of a child in a man's body; a big St. Bernard.

—Virginia Berry

He played too much football with his helmet off.

—Lyndon Johnson, U.S. president

Jerry's the only man I ever knew who can't walk and chew gum at the same time.

—Lyndon Johnson

GARFIELD, JAMES ABRAM

1831-1881, twentieth U.S. president

He rushes into a fight with the horns of a bull and the skin of a rabbit.

—Jeremiah Black, American
cabinet officer

Garfield has an interest everwhere . . . but in the Kingdom of Heaven.

—Oliver P. Brown, in John M.
Taylor's *Garfield of Ohio:
The Available Man*

Thomas Corwin, governor, senator, Secretary of State, once bemoaned his reputation of "being funny" as a handicap to the Presidency. He advised General James Garfield, "Never make people laugh . . . If you would succeed in life you must be solemn—as an ass. All the great monuments are built over solemn asses." Garfield became President of the U.S.

—Thomas Corwin, U.S. senator

GRANT, ULYSSES SIMPSON

1822-1885, eighteenth U.S. president

He does not march, nor quite walk, but pitches along as if the next step would bring him on his nose.

—Richard Henry Dana,
poet and essayist

Early in 1869 the cry was for "no politicians" but the country did not mean "no brains."

—William Claflin, merchant,
governor of Massachusetts

... The people are tired of a man who has not an idea above a horse or a cigar ...

—Joseph Brown, U.S. public official

He combined great gifts with great mediocrity.

—Woodrow Wilson, U.S. president

HARDING, WARREN GAMALIEL

1865-1923, twenty-ninth U.S. president

He had a bungalow mind.

—Woodrow Wilson, U.S. president

the only man or child who wrote a simple declarative sentence with seven grammatical errors is dead.

—e.e. cummings, poet

I am not fit for this office and never should have been here.

—On himself

If you were a girl, Warren, you'd be in the family way all the time. You can't say no.

—Harding's father

If there ever was he-harlot, it was this same Warren G. Harding.

—William Allen White, author

... a tin horn politician with the manner of a rural corn doctor and the mien of a ham actor.

—H.L. Mencken, author and critic

Harding was not a bad man. He was just a slob.

—Alice Roosevelt Longworth, socialite

Harding became president as a result of mistaken identity. The Republican presidential convention was held in a smoke-filled room, and visibility was so poor that Harding was mistaken for Hoover.

—Richard Armour, author

Few deaths are unmingled tragedies. Harding's was not, he died in time.

—Samuel Hopkins Adams, author

Everybody's second choice.

—Anonymous

HARRISON, BENJAMIN
1833-1901, twenty-third U.S. president

He is a cold-blooded, narrow-minded, prejudiced, obstinate, timid old psalm-singing Indianapolis politician.

—Theodore Roosevelt, U.S. president

HARRISON, WILLIAM HENRY

1773-1841, ninth U.S. president

[An] active but shallow mind, a political adventurer not without talents but self-sufficient, vain and indiscreet.

—John Quincy Adams, U.S. president

I am the clerk of the Court of Common Pleas of Hamilton County at your service . . . Some folks are silly enough to have formed a plan to make a President of the U.S. out of this Clerk and Clod Hopper.

—On himself

> Let Van from his cooler of silver drink wine
> And lounge on his cushioned settee;
> Our man on his buckeye bench can recline
> Content with hard cider is he!

—Whig campaign song

HAYES, RUTHERFORD BIRCHARD

1822-1893, nineteenth U.S. president

Mr. Hayes came in by a majority of one, and goes out by unanimous consent.

—Anonymous

> Pa! Pa! please tell Ma
> Hayes is in the White House!
> Ha! Ha! Ha!

—Democratic slogan-song of 1876

"Rutherfraud" B. Hayes
His Fraudulency.
Boss Thief.

—Campaign invectives, 1876

He is a 3rd rate nonentity, whose only recommendation is that he is obnoxious to no one.

—Henry Adams, historian and writer

HOOVER, HERBERT CLARK
1874-1964, thirty-first U.S. president

Hoover isn't a stuffed shirt. But at times he can give the most convincing impersonation of a stuffed shirt you ever saw.

—Anonymous

Mellon pulled the whistle,
Hoover rang the bell
Wall Street gave the signal
And the country went to hell.

—Jingle of the Great Depression

A private meeting with Hoover is like sitting in a bath of ink.

—Henry Stimson, U.S. statesman

Facts to Hoover's brain are as water to a sponge; they are absorbed into every tiny interstice.

—Bernard M. Baruch, U.S. financier

If you put a rose in Hoover's hand it would melt.

—Gutzon Borglum, sculptor

JACKSON, ANDREW

1767-1845, seventh U.S. president

Incompetent both by his ignorance and by the fury of his passions.

—John Quincy Adams, U.S. president

King Andrew the First.

—Popular saying

Except [for] an enormous fabric of Executive power, the President has built up nothing . . . He goes for destruction, universal destruction.

—Henry Clay, statesman

General Jackson's mother was a COMMON PROSTI-TUTE, brought to this country by the British soldiers! She afterwards married a Mulatto Man, with whom she had several children, of which number GENERAL JACKSON IS ONE!

—Propaganda of 1828

Little advanced in civilization over the Indians with whom he made war.

—Elijah Hunt Mills,
U.S. senator

I feel much alarmed at the prospect of seeing General Jackson President. He is one of the most unfit men I know for such a place.

—Thomas Jefferson, U.S. president

JEFFERSON, THOMAS
1743-1826, third U.S. president

. . . a slur upon the moral government of the world.
—John Quincy Adams, U.S. president

He was a mixture of profound and sagacious observation, with strong prejudices and irritated passions.
—John Quincy Adams

The moral character of Jefferson was repulsive. Continually puling about liberty, equality and the degrading curse of slavery, he brought his own children to the hammer, and made money of his debaucheries.
—Alexander Hamilton, statesman

Go, wretch, resign the presidential chair,
Disclose thy secret measures, foul or fair,
Go, search with curious eye, for horned frogs,
Mid the wild wastes of Louisianian bogs;
Or, where Ohio rolls his turbid stream,
Dig for huge bones, thy glory and thy theme.
Go, scan, Philosophist, thy [Sally's] charms
And sink supinely in her sable arms;
But quit to abler hands the helm of state,
Nor image ruin on thy country's fate!
—William Cullen Bryant, poet

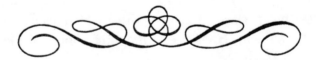

JOHNSON, ANDREW

1808-1875, seventeenth U.S. president

What will the aristocrats do, with a railsplitter for President, and a tailor for Vice President.

—On himself

[He] reduced the Presidency to the level of a grog house.

—John Sherman, statesman

Let them impeach and be damned!

—On himself

He is surrounded, hampered, tangled in the meshes of his own wickedness. Unfortunate, unhappy man, behold your doom!

—Thaddeus Stevens, U.S. congressman

JOHNSON, LYNDON BAINES

1908-1973, thirty-sixth US. President

When all the returns are in, perhaps President Johnson will have to settle for being recognized as the greatest American President for the poor and for the Negroes, but that, as I see it, is a very great honor indeed.

—Ralph Ellison, American writer

His skin is a millionth of an inch thick.

—Barry M. Goldwater, U.S. senator

. . . a riverboat gambler.

—John F. Kennedy, U.S. president

KENNEDY, JOHN FITZGERALD
1917-1963, thirty-fifth U.S. president

Jack Kennedy's father: Jack, what do you want as a career?
Jack Kennedy: I want to be president.
Jack Kennedy's father: I know that—but I mean when you grow up.

—Republican National Committee magazine

I sincerely fear for my country if Jack Kennedy should be elected president. The fellow has absolutely no principles. Money and gall are all the Kennedys have.

—Barry M. Goldwater, U.S. senator

There is a lot of he-coon ingrained in the hide of the new President. He strikes me as practically cold all the way, with a hard blue eye on Valhalla.

—Robert Ruark, author

That fucking bastard, he—wasn't supposed to use notes!

—Richard Nixon, then U.S. vice-
president, offstage after a Kennedy-
Nixon television debate in which
Nixon spoke of the dignity
of the presidency

LINCOLN, ABRAHAM
1809-1865, sixteenth U.S. president

. . . This man's appearance, his pedigree, his coarse low jokes and anecdotes, his vulgar similes and his frivolity, are a disgrace to the seat he holds. . . .

—John Wilkes Booth, actor

His mind works in the right directions but seldom works clearly and cleanly. His bread is of unbolted flour, and much straw, too, mixes in the bran, and sometimes gravel stones.

—Henry Ward Beecher,
clergyman and orator

He said to me that his father taught him to work, but he never taught him to love it.

—John Romaine, author

I claim not to have controlled events, but confess plainly that events have controlled me.

—On himself

He is a huckster in politics; a 1st-rate 2nd-rate man.

—Wendell Phillips, abolitionist

In Washington the most striking thing is the absence of personal loyalty to the President. It does not exist. He has no admirers, no enthusiastic supporters, none to bet on his head.

—Richard Henry Dana, American
lawyer and writer

My policy is to have no policy.

—On himself

Lincoln is now popularly known for being "heads" when one is matching pennies.

—Richard Armour, author

Filthy Story-Teller, Despot, Liar, Thief, Braggart, Buffoon, Usurper, Monster, Ignoramus, Old Scoundrel, Perjurer, Robber, Swindler, Tyrant, Field-Butcher, Land-Pirate.

—*Harper's Weekly*

The president is nothing more than a well-meaning baboon . . . I went to the White House directly after tea where I found "the original Gorilla" about as intelligent as ever. What a specimen to be at the head of our affairs now.

—Anonymous

By whom hath the Constitution been made obsolete?
By Abraham Africanus the First.
To what end?
That his day may be long in office—that he may make himself and his people the equal of the Negroes.
What is a President?
A general agent for Negroes.
Is it disloyal to honestly believe in one's heart that if Lincoln is not a fool he is a knave, and that if he is not a knave, he is a fool?
It is, horribly disloyal.
Who is Mrs. Lincoln?
The wife of the government.
Who is Mr. Lincoln?
A successful contractor to supply the government with mules.
Who is Master Bob Lincoln?
A lucky boy, yet in his teens, who has been so happy, as to obtain shares in Governments Contracts by which he has realized $30,000.

—Questions and Answers from the *Lincoln Catechism*, J.F. Fecks, Publisher

MADISON, JAMES

1751-1836, fourth U.S. president

Jemmy Madison—Oh, poor Jemmy, he is but a withered little applejohn.

—Washington Irving, author

Our President, though a man of amiable manners and great talents, has not, I fear, those commanding talents which are necessary to control those about him.

—John Calhoun, U.S. vice-president

McKINLEY, WILLIAM

1843-1901, twenty-fifth U.S. president

McKinley keeps his ear to the ground so close that he gets it full of grasshoppers much of the time.

—Joseph Cannon, Speaker of
House of Representatives

. . . had about as much backbone as a chocolate eclair.

—Theodore Roosevelt, U.S. president

Why, if a man were to call my dog McKinley and the brute failed to resent to the death the damning insult, I'd drown it.

—William Cowper Brann,
American journalist

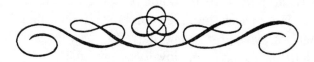

MONROE, JAMES

1758-1831, fifth U.S. president

His virtue was not in flying high but in walking orderly, his talents were exercised not in grandeur but in mediocrity.

—Arthur Styron, author

NIXON, RICHARD MILHOUS

1913-   , thirty-seventh U.S. president

* Tricky Dick—the Human Edsel
* Slippery Dick
* Nixon + Spiro = Zero
* Would You Let Your Sister Marry this Man?
* Would You Buy a Used Car from this Man?
* Dick is four-letter word.

—Campaign epithets

Sir Richard, the Chicken-Hearted.

—Hubert H. Humphrey, U.S. vice-president

Mr. Nixon may be very good in kitchen debates, but so are a great many other married men I know.

Last Thursday night Mr. Nixon dismissed me as "another Truman." I regard this as a compliment. I consider him another Dewey.

—John F. Kennedy, U.S. president

He is humorless to the point of being inhuman. He is devious. He is vacillating. He is profane. He is willing to be led. He displays dismaying gaps in knowledge. He is suspicious of his staff. His loyalty is minimal.

—Chicago *Tribune*

The Watergate transcripts revealed deplorable, disgusting, shabby, immoral performances by everyone involved, not excluding the President.

—Hugh Scott, U.S. Senate
Minority Leader

All right. They still call me "Tricky Dick." It's a brutal thing to fight. The carefully cultivated impression is that Nixon is devious. I can overcome this impression in one way only: by absolute candor.

—On himself

I believe that I spent too much time in the last campaign on substance and too little time on appearance; I paid too much attention to what I was going to say and too little to how I would look.

—On himself

You won't have Nixon to kick around any more, because, gentlemen, this is my last press conference.

—On himself, after his unsuccessful
attempt to become governor
of California

I made my mistakes, but in all my years of public life I have never profited, *never* profited from public service. I have earned every cent. And in all of my years of public life I have never obstructed justice. And I think, too, that I could say that in my years of public life that I welcome this kind of examination because people have got to know whether or not their President is a crook. Well, I am not a crook.

—On himself, during the
Watergate crisis

Nixonland is a land of slander and scare, of lay innuendo, of a poison pen and the anonymous telephone call, and hustling, pushing, and shoving—the land of smash and grab and anything to win.

—Adlai E. Stevenson, U.S. presidential candidate and statesman

Nixon went into politics the way other young men home from the war went into construction, or merchandising, or whatever—for lack of anything better to do . . . The fact is that as a candidate for office, Nixon has consistently been a thoroughly 2nd-rate politician, because he was made, not born.

—Stewart Alsop, columnist

Dick had two left feet. He couldn't coordinate. But boy, was he an inspiration. That's why the coach let him hang around, I guess. He was one of these inspirational guys.

—Member of the Whittier College football team

I'd love to see Ike's face when he finds out that Tricky Dick, his partner in the fight against Democratic corruption, has been on the take for the last 2 years . . . This should blow that moralizing, unscrupulous, double-dealing son-of-a-bitch right out of the water.

—James Wechsler, journalist

There is built into Nixon an automatic response mechanism triggered by opposition. Offer him the element of competition, tempt him with a fight, hint that someone might want to deprive him of some prize, and a tiger emerges from the camouflage he normally shows the world.

—Leonard Lurie, writer

He is the kind of politician who would cut down a redwood tree, then mount the stump and make a speech for conservation.

—Adlai E. Stevenson, statesman

Nixon is a shifty-eyed goddamm liar, and people know it. He's one of the few in the history of this country to run for high office talking out of both sides of his mouth at the same time and lying out of both sides.

—Harry S Truman, U.S. president

Tell us a dog story, Dick!

—Heckler teasing Nixon about his Checkers speech

When we're elected, we'll take care of people like you! . . . . OK boys, throw him out!

—Nixon, to his Secret Service men

There are very few of the human juices in Nixon. You like him. You admire him. But not because you feel that he loves you . . . . I mean, I always knew that in a showdown, if my friendship with Nixon were embarrassing to him, that he'd just let me go.

—Ralph deToledano, writer

One has the uneasy feeling that he is always on the verge of pronouncing himself the victim of some clandestine plot.

—Arthur Schlesinger, historian

He has no taste.

—John F. Kennedy, U.S. president

Nobody could talk like that and be normal.

> —John F. Kennedy, following Nixon's
> famous statement to the press after
> his loss of the gubernatorial race
> in California: "You won't have
> Nixon to kick around anymore."

. . . sick, sick, sick.

> —John F. Kennedy

Anyone who can't beat Nixon doesn't deserve to be president.

> —John F. Kennedy

I can't stand the way he puts everything in Tricia's mouth. It makes me sick. He's a cheap bastard; that's all there is to it.

> —John F. Kennedy's comment
> on Nixon's book *Six Crises*

PIERCE, FRANKLIN
1804-1869, fourteenth U.S. president

Many persons have difficulty remembering what President Franklin Pierce is best remembered for, and he is therefore probably best forgotten.

> —Richard Armour, author

Whoever may be elected, we cannot get a poorer cuss than now disgraces the Presidential Chair!

> —B.B. French

Frank, I pity you—indeed I do, from the bottom of my heart!

> —Nathaniel Hawthorne, author

POLK, JAMES KNOX

1795-1849, eleventh U.S. president

Polk's mind was rigid, narrow, obstinate, far from first-rate . . . But he knew how to get things done, which is the 1st necessity of Government, and he knew what he wanted done, which is the second.

—Bernard DeVoto, author

ROOSEVELT, FRANKLIN DELANO

1882-1945, thirty-second U.S. president

Roosevelt is my shepherd, I am in want.
He maketh me to lie down on park benches;
He leadeth me beside the still factories.
He disturbeth my soul:
He leadeth me in the Paths of destruction for
  his Party's sake.
Yea, though I walk through the valley of recession,
I anticipate no recovery
For he is with me;
His promises and pipe dreams they no longer fool
  me.
He prepareth a reduction in my salary in the
  presence of my creditors;
He anointeth my small income with taxes;
Surely unemployment and poverty shall follow me
  all the days of the New Deal
And I will dwell in a mortgaged house forever.

—anti-New Deal slogan

I'd rather be right than Roosevelt.
—Heywood Campbell Broun, columnist

I have always found Roosevelt an amusing fellow, but I would not employ him, except for reasons of personal friendship, as a geek in a common carnival.
—Murray Kempton, political columnist

. . . two-thirds mush and one-third Eleanor.
—Alice Roosevelt Longworth, socialite

ROOSEVELT, THEODORE
1858-1919, twenty-sixth U.S. president

Now look, that damned cowboy is President of the United States.
—Mark Hanna, American capitalist and politician

Heckler: I'm a Democrat.
TR: May I ask the gentleman why he is a Democrat?
Heckler: My grandfather was a Democrat; my father was a Democrat; and I am a Democrat.
TR: My friend, suppose your grandfather has been a jackass and your father was a jackass, what would you be?
Heckler: (quickly) A Republican.

❀ ❀ ❀

He hated all pretension save his own pretension.
—H.L. Mencken, author and critic

Theodore Roosevelt thought with his hips.
—Lincoln Steffens, editor and author

When Theodore attends a wedding, he wants to be the bride and when he attends a funeral, he wants to be the corpse.

—a relative

TAFT, WILLIAM HOWARD
1857-1930, twenty-seventh U.S. president

Taft has served so long under Theodore Roosevelt as a trouble shooter and yes-man that he never recovered from the subordinate experience . . . When someone addressed him as "Mr. President," he would instinctively turn around to see where Roosevelt was.

—Thomas A. Bailey, author

Politics, when I am in it, makes me sick.

—On himself

It's very difficult for me to understand how a man who is so good as Chief Justice could have been so bad as President.

—Louis Brandeis, Supreme Court Justice

Taft meant well, but he meant well feebly.

—Theodore Roosevelt, U.S. president

TAYLOR, ZACHARY
1784-1850, twelfth U.S. president

. . . quite ignorant for his rank, and quite bigoted in his ignorance . . . few men have ever had a more comfortable, labor-saving contempt for learning of every kind.

—Winfield Scott, American general

I am a Whig, but not an ultra-Whig.

—On himself

His nomination is a plot to deprive me of his society and to shorten his life by unnecessary care and responsibility.

—Mrs. Zachary Taylor, wife
of the president

TRUMAN, HARRY S

1884-1972, thirty-third U.S. president

Among President Truman's many weaknesses was his utter inability to discriminate between history and histrionics.

—Anonymous

To err is Truman.

—Repulican slogan

Mr. Truman is not performing, and gives no evidence of his ability to perform, the function of the Commander-in-Chief. At the very center of the Truman Administration there is a vacuum of responsibility and authority.

—Walter Lippman, critic

I don't care how the thing is explained. It defies all common sense to send that roughneck ward politician back to the White House.

—Robert Taft, U.S. senator

You can't make a President out of a ribbon clerk.

—Al Whitney, educator

In the middle of the speech, some big voice up in the corner hollered out, "Give 'em hell Harry!" Well, I never gave anybody hell; I just told the truth on these fellows and they thought it was hell.

—On himself

Ninety-six percent of 6,926 communists, fellow travelers, sex perverts, people with criminal records, dope addicts, drunks and other security risks removed under the Eisenhower security program were hired by the Truman Administration.

—Richard M. Nixon, during the
McCarthy period when Nixon
was a congressman

Even a Chinaman could beat Truman.

—Campaign slogan from 1948

The son-of-a-bitch ought to be impeached [for firing MacArthur].

—Joseph McCarthy, U.S. senator

A two-bit President of a five-star general.

—Anonymous

Harry Truman proves the old adage that any man can become President of the United States.

—Norman Thomas, socialist leader

TYLER, JOHN
1790-1862, tenth U.S. president

His Accidency.
The Accidental President.
Tyler Grippe.
Tippecanoe—but not Tyler too!
The Executive Ass.

           o   o   o

Do you know a traitor viler, viler, viler
Than Tyler?
> —Popular epithets spread by
> admirers of Henry Clay

Tyler is a political sectarian of the slave-driving, Virginia Jeffersonian school, principled against all improvement, with all the interests and passions and vices of slavery rooted in his moral and political constitution.
> —John Quincy Adams, U.S. president

He looked somewhat worn and anxious, and well he might be, being at war with everybody.
> —Charles Dickens, author

VAN BUREN, MARTIN
1782-1862, eighth U.S. president

While Harrison marched to the border,
Sly Van stayed at home as you know;
Afraid of the smell of gun-powder—
Then hurrah for Old Tippecanoe!

Ole Tip, he wears a homespun shirt,
He has no ruffled shirt, wirt, wirt.
But Matt, he has the golden plate,
And he's a little squirt, wirt, wirt.

—Whig song

Van Buren was not reelected, but his campaign was so hilarious that he was popularly acclaimed the Panic of 1837.

—Richard Armour, author

He is not . . . of the race of the lion or the tiger; he belongs to a lower order: the fox.

—John C. Calhoun, statesman

° Martin the First: King of North America
° Vanocracy
° Down with Van Burenism!

—Whig slogans

He rowed to his object with muffled oars.

—John Randolph, U.S.
statesman and orator

WASHINGTON, GEORGE

1732-1799, first U.S. president

The man who is the source of all the misfortunes of our country.

—William Duane, journalist

. . . and as to you, Sir, treacherous in private friendship . . . and a hypocrite in public life, the world will be puzzled to decide whether you are an apostate or an imposter, whether you have abandoned good principles, or whether you ever had had any.

—Thomas Paine, political writer

My movements to the chair of Government will be accompanied by feelings not unlike those of a culprit who is going to the place of his execution.

—On himself

He is too illiterate, unread, unlearned for his station and reputation.

—John Adams, U.S. president

His mind was slow in operation, but sure in conclusion . . . Hearing all suggestions, he selected whatever was best, but was slow in readjustment.

—Thomas Jefferson, U.S. president

Washington is the last person you'd ever suspect of having been a young man.

—Samuel Eliot Morison, historian

That dark designing sordid ambitious vain proud arrogant and vindictive knave.

—Charles Lee, Revolutionary
Army general

WILSON, (THOMAS) WOODROW

1856-1924, twenty-eighth U.S. president

The air currents of the world never ventilated his mind.

—Walter Hines Page, journalist
and diplomat

I feel certain that he would not recognize a generous impulse if he met it on the street.

—William Howard Taft,
U S president

How can I talk to a fellow who thinks himself the first man in two thousand years to know anything about peace on earth?

—Georges Clemenceau,
French premier

Mr. Wilson bores me with his Fourteen Points; why God Almighty has only ten.

—Arthur Link, critic

He had to hold the reins and do the driving alone; it was the only kind of leadership he knew.

—Arthur Link

He is an utterly selfish and cold-blooded politician always.

—Theodore Roosevelt, U S president

A Byzantine logothete.

—Theodore Roosevelt

Chapter Two

····

PRIME MINISTERS, STATESMEN, AND OTHER POLITICOS

The British House of Commons has always afforded members of Parliament—and especially the prime minister who headed the government—an opportunity to vent their frustrations, anger, and dislikes at the government. But Parliament also gave the prime minister a good and clear shot at the opposition. When the prime minsters were of the caliber of a Gladstone or a Disraeli and played musical chairs in heading the government, a genuine potpourri of insults ensued. Disraeli in the nineteenth and Churchill in the twentieth century were masters of the quick and sharp repartee. But others were also no mean practitioners of the art.

According to some, a statesman is a politician who manages to keep the illusion of clean hands. Cynics claim they are birds of a feather.

The expression of disdain for politicians dates back to ancient times, but in our era it has been raised to a fine art.

Even politicians who are later held up in history books as heroes of their nations are reviled in their time as dishonest, untrustworthy men, masters of the broken promise, proponents of false and dangerous programs, craftsmen in reaching their hands into the public till, sadistic experts in raising taxes and irresponsibly spending money.

Many of the insults below reflect this low esteem.

ACHESON, DEAN G.

1893-1971, U.S. government official

I watch his smart-aleck manner and his British clothes and that New Dealism, everlasting New Dealism in everything he says and does, and I want to shout "Get out, get out. You stand for everything that has been wrong with the United States for years."

—Hugh Butler, U.S. senator

ADAMS, SAMUEL

1722-1803, Revolutionary statesman

Every dip of his pen stung like a horned snake.

—Sir Francis Bernard, British
colonial governor

I shall . . . give you a sketch of some of Mr. Samuel Adams's features, and I do not know how to delineate them stronger than by the observation made by a celebrated painter in America, viz., "That if he wished to draw the picture of the devil, that he would get Sam Adams to sit for him."

—Peter Oliver, author

ADDINGTON, HENRY, VISCOUNT SIDMOUTH
1757-1844, British prime minister and statesman

Clothed with the Bible, as with light,
And the shadows of the night,
Like Sidmouth, next Hypocrisy
On a crocodile rode by.

—Percy Bysshe Shelley, poet

The indefinable air of a village apothecary inspecting the tongue of the State.

—Lord Archibald Rosebery,
statesman and author

ASQUITH, HERBERT HENRY,
EARL OF OXFORD AND ASQUITH
1852-1928, British prime minister

. . .black and wicked and with only a nodding acquaintance with the truth.

—Lady Cunard

My colleagues tell military secrets to their wives, except X who tells them to other people's wives.

—Lord Horatio Kitchener, British
field marshall and statesman

When one has peeled off the brown-paper wrapping of phrases and compromises, one finds—just nothing at all.

—Lytton Strachey,
biographer and critic

ASTOR, NANCY WITCHER, VISCOUNTESS

1879-1964, first female member of British Parliament

> *Quick exchange between Lady Astor and Winston Churchill:*
> *Astor:* Winston, if you were my husband, I should flavor your coffee with poison.
> *Churchill:* Madam, if I were your husband, I should drink it.

✿   ✿   ✿

Viscount Waldorf Astor owned Britain's two most influential newspapers, *The Times* and the *Observer*, but his American wife, Nancy, had a wider circulation than both papers put together.

—Emery Klein, author

Nannie was a devout Christian Scientist, but not a good one. She kept confusing herself with God. She didn't know when to step aside and give God a chance.

—Mrs. Gordon Smith, in Elizabeth Langhorne's *Nancy Astor and Her Friends*

ATTLEE, CLEMENT RICHARD, EARL ATTLEE

1883-1967, British prime minister

He seems determined to make a trumpet sound like a tin whistle . . . He brings to the fierce struggle of politics the tepid enthusiasm of a lazy summer afternoon at a cricket match.

—Aneurin Bevan, political leader

A modest little man with much to be modest about.

—Aneurin Bevan

He is a sheep in sheep's clothing.

—Winston Churrchill, British
prime minister

BACON, FRANCIS, VISCOUNT ST. ALBANS

1561-1626, philosopher, statesman

Whenn their lordships asked Bacon
How many bribes he had taken
He had at least the grace
To get red in the face.

—Edmund Clerihew Bentley, author

Lord Bacon could as easily have created the planets as he could have written *Hamlet*.

—Thomas Carlyle, Scottish historian,
philosopher, and essayist

Some people think that physics was invented by Sir Francis Bacon, who was hit by an apple when he was sitting under a tree one day writing Shakespeare.

—Eric Larrabee, author

His faults were—we write it with pain—coldness of heart, and meanness of spirit. He seems to have been incapable of feeling strong affection, of facing great dangers, of making great sacrifices.

—T.B. Macaulay, historian, poet,
essayist, and statesman

BALDWIN, STANLEY, EARL OF BEWDLEY
1867-1947, British prime minister

I think Baldwin has gone mad. He simply takes one jump in the dark; looks around; and then takes another.
—Lord Frederick Birkenhead,
statesman and jurist

I see no point in swapping donkeys when crossing a stream.
—Lord Frederick Birkenhead

BARÈRE, BERTRAND
1755-1841, French Jacobin demagogue

. . . Barère approached nearer than any person mentioned in history or fiction, whether man or devil, to the idea of consummate and universal depravity. In him the qualities which are the proper objects of hatred, and the qualities which are the proper objects of contempt preserve an exquisite and absolute harmony.
—T.B. Macaulay, historian, poet,
essayist, and statesman

BARING, EVELYN, EARL OF CROMER
1841-1917, statesman

His temperament, all in monochrome, touched in with cold blues and indecisive greys, was eminently unromantic.
—Lytton Strachey, biographer
and critic

BEGIN, MENACHEM

1913-   , Israeli prime minister

"[Begin] is like a man who steals your cow. You ask for it back, and he demands a ransom."

—Anwar Sadar,
president of Egypt

BENTHAM, JEREMY

1748-1832, political theorist

The arch-philistine Jeremy Bentham was the insipid, pedantic, leather-tongued oracle of the bourgeois intelligence of the Nineteenth Century.

—Karl Marx, philosopher
and socialist writer

BENTON, THOMAS HART

1792-1858, politician

. . . [He was] the greatest of all humbugs, and could make more out of nothing than any other man in the world. He ought to have gone about all his life with quack doctors, and written puffs for their medicines. Had he done so, he might have made a fortune.

—John C. Calhoun, U.S. vice-president

. . . a liar of magnitude.

—John Quincy Adams, U.S. president

Colonel Benton has read a good deal; but his mind is like a baggage wagon, full of all kinds of lumber . . . His imagination is a sort of Cyclops' great sledge hammer, heavy, weighty, crushing, iron-wrought.

—Anonymous

A house lamb and a street lion.

—On himself

BEVIN, ERNEST
1881-1951, statesman

Bevin thought he was Palmerston wearing Keir Hardie's cloth cap, whereas he was really the Foreign Office's Charlie McCarthy.

—Konni Zilliacus, author

He objected to ideas only when others had them.

—A.J.P. Taylor, author

BIRKENHEAD, EARL OF
(FREDERICK EDWIN SMITH)
1872-1930, statesman

. . . a man with the vision of an eagle but with a blind spot in his eye.

—Andrew Bonar Law, British
prime minister

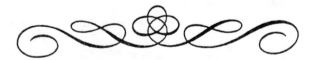

BLAINE, JAMES GILLESPIE

1830-1893, statesman

> For ways that are dark
> And tricks that are vain,
> I name Speaker Blaine
> And that I dare maintain.
>
> —Benjamin F. Butler, Union
> general, lawyer, and
> politician

Wallowing in corruption like a rhinoceros in an African pool.

—Edwin L. Godkin, editor

> Blaine! Blaine! J.G. Blaine
> Continental Liar from the State of Maine.
>
> —Anonymous campaign slogan of 1884

BOLINGBROKE, VISCOUNT (HENRY ST. JOHN)

1768-1751, statesman

When he was appointed Minister, a woman of the streets was said to have cried: "Seven thousand guineas a year, my girls, and all for us!"

—Michael Foot, author

BORAH, WILLIAM EDGAR

1865-1940, U.S. senator

His career is notable in a hundred ways and celebrated in none.

—Anonymous

. . . he was always winding himself up, but never struck twelve.

—Anonymous

BROWN, EDMUND G. (PAT)

1905-   , governor of California

Tell me, why do all you guys from the eastern newspapers always refer to Pat Brown as a bumbling horse's ass?

—On himself

BRYAN, WILLIAM JENNINGS

1860-1925, American statesman, orator, and reformer

His mind was like a soup dish: wide and shallow. It could hold a small amount of nearly anything,   but the slightest jarring spilled the soup into somebody's lap.

—Irving Stone, author

What a disgusting, dishonest fakir Bryan is! When I see so many Americans running after him, I feel very much as I do when a really lovely woman falls in love with a cad.

—Elihu Root, politician

A kindly man and well meaning in a weak kind of way.

—Theodore Roosevelt, U.S. president

One could drive a prairie schooner through any part of his argument and never scrape against a fact.

—David F. Houston, American
cabinet officer and educator

. . . a halfbaked glib little briefless jack-leg lawyer . . .

—John Milton Hay, U.S. secretary
of state and writer

. . . money-grabbing, selfish, office-seeking, favour-hunting, publicity-loving, marplot from Nebraska.

—Anonymous

BUCKINGHAM, FIRST DUKE OF (GEORGE VILLIERS)

1592-1628, statesman, royal favorite

Who rules the Kingdom? The King!
Who rules the King? The Duke!
Who rules the Duke? The Devil!

—Anonymous

But it is generally given to him who is the little god at court, to be the great devil in the country. The commonality hated him with a perfect hatred; and all miscarriages in Church and State, at home, abroad, at sea and land, were charged on his want of wisdom, valour, or loyalty

—Thomas Fuller, English
clergyman and author

BURR, AARON

1756-1836, politician, U.S. vice-president

Burr was practiced in every art of gallantry; he had made womankind a study. He never saw a beautiful face and form without a sort of restless desire to experiment upon it and try his power over the inferior inhabitant.

—Harriet Beecher Stowe, author

This man has no principles, public or private. As a politician, his sole spring of action is an inordinate ambition.

—Alexander Hamilton, first U.S.
secretary of the treasury

. . . a cold-blooded Catalin . . . a profligate; a voluptuary . . . without doubt insolvent.

—Alexander Hamilton

Oh Burr, oh Burr, what has thout done,
Thou hast shooted dead great Hamilton!
You hid among a bund of thistle,
And shooted him dead with a great hoss pistol!

—Anonymous poem current after
famous pistol duel in which
Burr killed Hamilton (1804)

Aaron Burr—may his treachery to his country exalt him to the scaffold, and hemp be his escort to the republic of dust and ashes.

—Anonymous

CALHOUN, JOHN CALDWELL

1782-1850, statesman, U.S. vice-president

Mr. Speaker! I mean Mr. President of the Senate and would-be President of the United States, which God in His infinite mercy avert.

—John Randolph, statesman

. . . a smart fellow, one of the first among second-rate men, but of lax political principles and a disordinate ambition not over-delicate in the means of satisfying itself.

—Albert Gallatin, American financier
and public official

. . . hang him as high as Haman.

—Andrew Jackson, U.S. president

The sabled genius of the South who opposed Northern property.

—John Quincy Adams, U.S. president

CAMPBELL, JOHN, BARON
1779-1861, jurist

Edinburgh is now celebrated for having given us the two greatest bores that have ever yet been known in London, for Jack Campbell in the House of Lords is just what Tom Macaulay is in private society.

—Lord Henry Brougham, statesman

CHAMBERLAIN, (ARTHUR) NEVILLE
1869-1940, British prime minister

Look at his head. The worst thing Neville Chamberlain ever did was to meet Hitler and let Hitler see him.

—David Lloyd George, British
prime minister

He looked at foreign affairs through the wrong end of a municipal drainpipe.

—Winston Churchill, British
prime minister

CHAMBERLAIN, JOSEPH
1836-1914, statesman

He was not born, bred or educated in the ways which alone secure the necessary tact and behaviour of a real gentleman.
—Sir Edward Hamilton, statesman

Mr. Chamberlain who looked and spoke like a cheesemonger.
—Benjamin Disraeli, British prime minister

Mr. Chamberlain loves the working man; he loves to see him work.
—Anonymous

CHASE, SALMON PORTLAND
1808-1873, politician

Chase is a good man, but his theology is unsound. He thinks there is a fourth person in the Trinity.
—Anonymous

CHESTERFIELD, EARL OF
1694-1773, courtier and statesman

On Lord Chesterfield's published letters of advice to his son: They inculcate the morals of a whore, and the manners of a dancing master.
—Samuel Johnson, writer, critic, and lexicographer

The only Englishman who ever argued for the art of pleasing as the first duty of life.

—Voltaire, French satirist, philosopher
dramatist, and historian

CHURCHILL, LORD RANDOLPH (HENRY SPENCER)

1849-1895, statesman

Did you ever know a man who, having had a boil on his neck, wanted another?

—Lord Robert Salisbury, statesman

CHURCHILL, WINSTON

1874-1965, British prime minister

Why should I question the monkey when I can question the organ grinder?

—Aneurin Bevan,
political leader

CLAY, HENRY

1777-1852, statesman and orator

Adams, Clay and Company. Would to God they were like Jonah in the Whale's belly; and the door locked, key lost, and not a son of Vulcan within a million miles to make another.

—Anonymous

I have only two regrets: that I have not shot Henry Clay or hanged John C. Calhoun.

—Andrew Jackson, U.S. president

An accidental meeting on a narrow sidewalk in Washington between Henry Clay and John Randolph:

Clay: I, Sir, do not step aside for a scoundrel.

Randolph: On the other hand, I always do.

o   o   o

. . . . like a mackerel in the moonlight; he shines and he stinks.

—John Randolph, U.S. congressman

> Oh, coony, coony Clay,
>   the rich man is your god—
> You raise the Manufacturer,
>   But doom the poor to plod.

—Democratic campaign song

He is like almost all the eminent men of this country, only half educated. His morals, public and private, are loose.

—John Quincy Adams, U.S. president

CONNALLY, JOHN R.

1917-   , U.S. politician

John Connally in the White House would be a nightmare . . . when it comes between, say, ambition and honor, it will be ambition that will win out; when it comes between ethics and victory, ethics is going to lose.

—Henry Gonzales, U.S. congressman

The good Lord chose to leave me here, so I feel that instead off being elected, maybe I'm one of God's elect.

—On himself

I don't like him and I don't trust him.

—Roy Wilkins, executive secretary
to the NAACP

He was the worst, most reactionary and vicious governor in Texas history . . . He was just nasty and vindictive . . .He wouldn't cooperate with our congressional delegation or leaders back home. It was pathetic.

—Ralph Yarborough, U.S senator

COX, JACK
1921-   , Texas politician

A renegade, turncoat opportunist.

—John R. Connally, governor of Texas,
after Cox, in 1962, changed
his party loyalty from
Democrat to Republican

CRIPPS, SIR STAFFORD
1889-1952, British statesman

There, but for the grace of God, goes God.

—Winston Churchill, British
prime minister

CROMWELL, OLIVER
1599-1658, English general and statesman

He lived a hypocrite and died a traitor.

—John Foster, clergyman and essayist

CURTIS, CARL
1905-   , U.S. senator

I can't see [comprehend] Curtis. He can't talk. He's unprepossessing. And he's generally shit.
—John F. Kennedy, U.S. president

DAVIS, JEFFERSON
1808-1889, president of the Confederacy

Yes, I know Mr. Davis. He is as ambitious as Lucifer, cold as a snake, and what he touches will not prosper.
—Sam Houston, soldier and politician

DEWEY, THOMAS E.
1902-19711, governor of New York

I know Gov. Thomas E. Dewey and Mr. Dewey is a fine man. Yes, Dewey is a fine man. So is my Uncle Morris. My Uncle Morris shouldn't be president; neither should Dewey.
—George Jessel, comedian

He is small and insignificant, and he makes too much of an effort, with his forced smile and jovial manner, to impress himself upon people. To me he is a political streetwalker accosting men with "come home with me, dear."
—Harold L. Ickes, U.S. secretary
of the interior

You can't make a soufflé rise twice.
—Alice Roosevelt Longworth,
socialite

You really have to get to know Dewey to dislike him.

—Alice Roosevelt Longworth

. . . the little man on the wedding cake.

—Alice Roosevelt Longworth

DIEFENBAKER, JOHN G.

1895-1979, Canadian prime minister

I did not write S.O.B. on the Rostow document . . . I didn't think Diefenbaker was a son of a bitch. I thought he was a prick.

—John F. Kennedy, U.S. president, after the prime minister accused Kennedy of writing S.O.B. on a State Department document referring to Diefenbaker

DIRKSEN, EVERETT

1896-1969, U.S. senator

The Wizard of Ooze.

—John F. Kennedy, alluding to his verbosity

DISRAELI, BENJAMIN

1804-1881, British prime minister

His life . . . is a living lie. He is the most degraded of his species and kind; and England is degraded in tolerating or having upon the face of her society a miscreant of his abominable, foul, and atrocious nature . . . . If there be harsher terms in the British language I should use them, because it is the harshest of all terms that would be descriptive of a wretch of his species.

—Daniel O'Connell, Irish
political leader

How long will John Bull allow this absurd monkey to dance on his chest?

—Thomas Carlyle, historian
and essayist

He is a self-made man and worships his creator.

—John Bright, English statesman
and political economist

DOBRYNIN, ANATOLI
1920-   , Soviet ambassador to Washington

I miss black bread and the cultural life.

—On himself, after 16
years in Washington

DODD, THOMAS J.
1907-1971, U.S. senator from Connecticut

Here's to the second nastiest drunk in town.

—Thomas O'Neill, U.S. congressman

DOUGLAS, STEPHEN ARNOLD
1813-1861, politician

As thin as the homeopathic soup that was made by boiling the shadow of a pigeon that had been starved to death.

—Abraham Lincoln, U.S president

. . . I did keep a grocery, and I did sell cotton, candles and cigars, and sometimes whiskey; but I remember in those days Mr. Douglas was one of my best customers. Many a time have I stood on one side of the counter and sold whiskey to Mr. Douglas on the other side, but the difference between us now is this: I have left my side of the counter, but Mr. Douglas still sticks to his tenaciously as ever.

—Abraham Lincoln

Douglas will cling to the Democratic banner as long as a *shred* is *left*; his party may kick him, beat him, but as long as he has a hope of being taken up as a candidate for the Presidency he will humble himself too *low* to be respected by his party.

—R.P. Letcher, lawyer and
Kentucky legislator

Douglas never can be president, Sir. No, Sir; Douglas never can be president, Sir. His legs are too short, Sir. His coat, like a cow's tail, hangs too near the ground, Sir.

—Thomas Hart Benton, statesman

His face was convulsed, his gesticulations frantic, and he lashed himself into such a heat that if his body had been made out of combustible matter, it would have burnt out. In the midst of his roaring to save himself from choking, he stripped off and cast away his cravat, and unbuttoned his waistcoat, and had the air and aspect of a half-naked pugilist. And this man comes from the judicial bench, and passes for an eloquent orator.

—John Quincy Adams, U.S. president

I could travel from Boston to Chicago by the light of my own effigies.

—On himself, commenting on the effigies burned across the country in response to his stance on slavery

EDEN, (ROBERT) ANTHONY
1897-1977, British prime minister

. . . an overripe banana, yellow outside, squishy inside.

—Reginald Paget

FRANKLIN, BENJAMIN
1706-1790, statesman, scientist

. . . a crafty and lecherous old hypocrite . . . whose very statue seems to gloat on the wenches as they walk the State House yard.

—William Cobbett, English journalist and reformer

When Franklin was seventy, he was sent to Paris to see what he could do to improve relations with the French, and he is said to have done extremely well despite his age. He died full of honors, *escargots*, *pâté*, and *vin rouge*.

—Richard Armour, author

The vulgarity he spread is still with us.

—Charles Angoff, author

He is our wise prophet of chicanery, the great buffoon, the face on the penny stamp.

—William Carlos Williams, author

A philosophical Quaker full of mean and thrifty maxims.

—John Keats, poet

Benjamin Franklin, incarnation of the peddling, tuppenny Yankee.

—Jefferson Davis, president
of the Confederacy

GAITSKELL, HUGH TODD NAYLOR
1906-1963, British statesman

A desiccated calculating machine.

—Aneurin Bevan, British
political leader

GARNER, JOHN NANCE
1869-1967, U.S. vice-president

He is a labor-baiting, poker-playing, whiskey-drinking, evil old man.

—John L. Lewis, labor leader

GARVEY, MARCUS MOZIAH
1887-1940, political organizer

. . . a bully with his own folk but servile in the presence of the Man, a sheer opportunist and a demagogic charlatan.

—Robert W. Gagnall, NAACP

It's a pity the cannibals do not get hold of this man.

—Anonymous

GLADSTONE, WILLIAM EWART

1809-1898, British prime minister

He was generally thought to be very pusillanimous in dealing with foreign affairs. That is not at all the impression I derived. He was wholly ignorant.

—Lord Evelyn Cromer, British
administrator in Egypt

Posterity will do justice to that unprincipled maniac Gladstone—extraordinary mixture of envy, vindictiveness, hypocrisy, and superstition; and with one commanding characteristic—whether Prime Minister, or Leader of Opposition, whether preaching, praying, speechifying or scribbling—never a gentleman!

—Benjamin Disraeli, British
prime minister

He has not a single redeeming defect.

—Benjamin Disraeli

When Gladstone yelled at Disraeli in the House of Commons, crying, "You, sir, will die either on the gallows or of some loathsome disease," Disraeli replied, "That, sir, depends upon whether I embrace your principles or your mistress."

—Benjamin Disraeli

If Gladstone fell into the Thames, that would be a misfortune, and if anybody pulled him out that, I suppose, would be a calamity.

—Benjamin Disraeli

A sophisticated rhetorician, inebriated with the exuberance of his own verbosity, and gifted with an egotistical imagination that can at all times command an interminable and inconsistent series of arguments to malign an opponent and glorify himself.

—Benjamin Disraeli

I don't object to the Old Man's always having the ace of trumps up his sleeve, but merely to his belief that God Almighty put it there.

—Henry du Pré Labouchere, British
politician and journalist

Gladstone appears to me one of the contemptiblest men I ever looked on . . . almost spectral kind of phantasm of a man—nothing in him but forms and ceremonies and outside wrappages; incapable of seeing veritably any fact whatever, but seeing, crediting, and laying to heart the mere clothes of the fact and fancying that all the rest does not exist. Let him fight his own battle, in the name of Beelzebub the god of Ekron, who seems to be his God. Poor phantasm!

—Thomas Carlyle, Scottish historian,
philosopher, and essayist

GOLDWATER, BARRY

1909-   U.S. senator, presidential candidate in 1964

Au H_2O + 1964 =   [the symbol of atomic explosion.]

—Anonymous

For Barry Goldwater, whom I urge to follow the career for which he has shown so much talent.

—John Kennedy, U.S. president, upon being asked by Goldwater to autograph a photograph he had taken of the president

GRASSO, ELLA
1919-   , governor of Connecticut

[I imagined her as] fat, sort of a sweaty thing.

—Lillian Carter, mother of President Jimmy Carter

Smella Ella.

—Anonymous

GRENVILLE, GEORGE
1712-1770, British prime minister

. . . a fatiguing orator and indefatigable drudge; more likely to disgust than offend. As all his passions were expressed by one livid smile, he never blushed at the variations in his behaviour . . . scarce any man ever wore in his face such outward and visible marks of the hollow, cruel, and rotten heart within.

—Horace Walpole, author

GREY, EDWARD, VISCOUNT GREY OF FALLODON
1862-1933, statesman

He was a mean man, . . .I am glad I trampled upon his carcass. He would have pursued me even from his grave.

—David Lloyd George, British
prime minister

GROMYKO, ANDREI
1909- , Russian official

Look at Gromyko—he'd sit two hours on a cake if I ordered him to.

—Nikita Khrushchev, Soviet leader

HALLEK, CHARLES A.
1900- , U.S. congressman

Trying to touch [convince] Charlie is like trying to pick up a greased pig.

—John F. Kennedy, U.S. president

HAMILTON, ALEXANDER
1757-1804, statesman, first U.S. secretary of the treasury

The bastard brat of a Scotch pedlar.

—John Adams, U.S. president

HAMPDEN, JOHN

1594-1643, statesman

He had a head to contrive, a tongue to persuade, and a hand to execute any mischief.

—Edward Hyde, author

HANCOCK, JOHN

1737-1793, merchant, politician

. . . John Hancock! A man without head and without heart—the mere shadow of a man!—and yet a Governor of Old Massachusetts.

—John Adams, U.S. president

HOPKINS, HARRY LLOYD

1890-1946, adviser to President Franklin D. Roosevelt

. . . he was generally regarded as a sinister figure, a backstairs intriguer, an Iowan combination of Machiavelli, Svengali and Rasputin.

—Robert E. Sherwood, dramatist

Mr. Hopkins is a bull-headed man whose high place in the New Deal was won by his ability to waste more money in quicker time on more absurd undertakings than any other mischievous wit in Washington could think of.

—Anonymous

HOUGHTON, BARON
(RICHARD MONCKTON MILNES)
1809-1885, politician, author

There is only one post fit for you, and that is the office of perpetual president of the Heaven and Hell Amalgamation Society.

—Thomas Carlyle, Scottish historian,
philosopher, and essayist

HUMPHREY, HUBERT H.
1911-1978, U.S. vice-president

One Democratic automobile, the Hubert, designed as the plain people's car, known as the Folks Wagon, has been withdrawn from the race, which is a pity, for it had acceleration. From a standing start, it could roar up to 300 words a minute in five seconds.

—Kenneth Keating, U.S. senator

HUNT, HENRY (ORATOR HUNT)
1773-1835, radical politician

. . . the incarnation of an empty, blustering, restless, ignorant, and selfish demagogue . . .

—-Harriet Martineau, author

ICKES, HAROLD

1874-1952, American statesman

The trouble with Ickes was . . . well, he was no better than a common cold. I don't like saying that about a man but it's true, and he wanted to be President the worst way.

—Harry S Truman, U.S. president

KENNEDY, EDWARD M. (TED)

1932-   , U.S. senator

A man can build a staunch reputation for honesty by admitting he was in error, especially when he gets caught at it.

—Robert Ruark, author

It won't go over with the WASPs. They take a very dim view of looking over your shoulder at someone else's exam paper. They go in more for stealing from stockholders and banks.

—John F. Kennedy, U.S. president, on learning
that his brother Ted, in his freshman
year at Harvard, had arranged for a
friend to take a foreign-language
exam for him. Both were asked
to leave college, but with a
provision that they could
reapply after an absence.
Both graduated in 1956.

KENNEDY, JOSEPH P.

1888-   , U.S. ambassador to England

[He was a] Chamberlain-umbrella policy man. [He] thought Hitler was right.

—Lyndon B. Johnson, U.S. senator, during the 1960 primary campaign

KENNEDY, ROBERT FRANCIS

1924-1968, U.S. Attorney-General, presidential campaign

. . . the highest-ranking withdrawn adolescent since Alexander Hamilton in 1794.

—Murray Kempton, newspaper columnist

That was the Kennedy way. You bit off more than you could chew, and then you chewed it.

—Gerald Gardner, author

LBJ always referred to Robert Kennedy in one way. He called him "the little shit." I'll buy that in spades although in that connection I wouldn't have called him "little."

That incident [in Hoffa's office] turned out to be the start of what was to become a blood feud. Maybe it didn't seem like much at the time, but I had stepped on a poison snake [Robert Kennedy].

—Jimmy Hoffa, president, Teamsters Union

KHRUSHCHEV, NIKITA

1894-1971, Soviet Communist leader

No pig-eyed bag of wind is going to push us out of Berlin.

—Frank L. Howley

KISSINGER, HENRY

1923   , U.S. secretary of state

You can't imagine how painful it was to see how much could be accomplished without me.

——On himself, after the Camp David peace talks between Carter, Sadat, and Begin

In a way, I'm glad to know the place I used to shit will be Henry's office.

—Bryce N. Harlow, President Nixon's aid who was compelled to give up his office bathroom to accommodate the enlargement of Kissinger's office

. . . an eel icier than ice.

—Oriana Fallaci, journalist

LA GUARDIA, FIORELLO HENRY

1882-1947, politician, mayor of New York City

If it's LaGuardia or bust, I prefer bust!

—Joseph M. Price, politician

LAW, ANDREW BONAR
1858-1923, British prime minister

It is fitting that we should have buried the Unknown Prime Minister by the side of the Unknown Soldier.

—Herbert Henry Asquith,
British prime minister

LIVERPOOL, EARL OF
(ROBERT BANKS JENKINSON)
1770-1828, British prime minister

Liverpool has acted as he always does to a friend in personal questions—shabbily, timidly and ill.

—Viscount Henry Palmerson,
British prime minister

LLOYD GEORGE, DAVID, EARL LLOYD GEORGE OF DWYFOR
1863-1945, British prime minister

He couldn't see a belt without hitting below it.

—Lady Margot Asquith, socialite
and author

He did not seem to care which way he travelled providing he was in the driver's seat.

—Lord William Beaverbrook, statesman
and newspaper publisher

LODGE, HENRY CABOT

1850-1924, U.S. senator, author

He was as cool as an undertaker at a hanging.

—H.L. Mencken, writer, editor,
and critic

A degenerate son of Harvard.

—A. Lawrence Lowell, lawyer
and president of Harvard

[Lodge had] a hard enough time keeping his temperr without stopping to consult his conscience.

—Thomas A. Bailey, author

LONG, HUEY PIERCE

1893-1935, politician, U.S. senator

He destroyed many things with his mind. And among them was himself.

—Raymond Moley, author

The trouble with Senator Long is that he is suffering from halitosis of the intellect. That's presuming Emperor Long has an intellect.

—Harold Ickes, U.S. secretary
of the interior

. . . like Huey Long who was later assassinated. He was a liar, and he was nothing but a damn demagogue. It didn't surprise me when they shot him. These demagogues, the ones that live by demagoguery. They all end up the same way.

—Harry S Truman, U.S. president

MacDONALD, (JAMES) RAMSAY
1866-1937, British prime minister

He has sufficient conscience to bother him, but not sufficient to keep him straight.

> —David Lloyd George, British prime minister

We know that he has, more than any other man, the gift of compressing the largest amount of words into the smallest amount of thought.

> —Winston Churchill, British
> prime minister

McCARTHY, JOSEPH
1908-57, politician, U.S. senator

McCarthy is the only major politician in the country who can be labelled "liar" without fear of libel.

> —Joseph and Stewart Alsop,
> syndicated columnists

I cussed out old McCarthy every chance I got. He was nothing but a damn coward, and he was afraid of me. The only thing he ever did that I approved of was when he knocked down Drew Pearson.

> —Harry S Truman, U.S. president

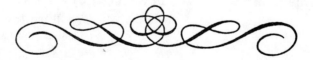

MITCHELL, MARTHA

1918-1977, wife of U.S. Attorney General John Mitchell, Washington gossip

It could have been a hell of a lot worse. They could have sentenced me to life with Martha Mitchell.

—John Mitchell, U.S. attorney general,
commenting on the jail sentence
he received for his Watergate
involvements

I tried to be a member of the Silent Majority but I felt like Martha Mitchell with a mouthful of Novocain.

—Liz Carpenter, social secretary
to Mrs. Lyndon Johnson

Men who could blow whole countries off the face of the earth . . . were powerless if Martha Mitchell reached for the phone.

—Eric Severaid, news analyst

She was called the mouth that roared and the "worst tressed" woman in America.

—from a review in *Time* magazine

MORSE, WAYNE LYMAN

1900-1974, U.S. senator

I am grateful for the overwhelming vote of confirmation in the Senate. We must now wait until the dirt settles. My difficulties, of course, go back for some years when Senator Wayne Morse was kicked in the head by a horse.

—Clare Booth Luce, U.S.
ambassador to Brazil

Any guy who can raise a horse like that, and ride like that, can't be the son of a—I always thought he was!

—Political opponent

MUNDT, KARL
1900-19   , U.S. senator

The Leaning Tower of Putty.

—Popular saying

NGUYEN, CAO KY
1930-   , former Vietnamese politician

I am not Americanized yet. I do not wash dishes.

—On himself, after settling
in the U.S.

NORTH, FREDERICK, EARL OF GUILFORD
1732-1792, British prime minister

Lord North was a coarse and heavy man, with a wide mouth, thick lips, and puffy cheeks, which seemed typical of his policy.

—J.H. Rose, English historian

O'CONNELL, DANIEL
1755-1847, Irish political leader

His fame blazed like a straw bonfire, and has left behind it scarce a shovelful of ashes. Never any public man had it in his power to do so much good for his country, nor was there ever one who accomplished so little.

—J.A. Froude, author

PALMERSTON, VISCOUNT
(HENRY JOHN TEMPLE)
1784-1865, British prime minister

Do the exact opposite of what [Palmerston] did. His administration at the Foreign Office was one long crime.

—John Bright, statesman and orator

You owe the Whigs great gratitude, my lord, and therefore, I think, you will betray them. Your lordship is like a favourite footman on easy terms with his mistress. Your dexterity seems a happy compound of the smartness of an attorney's clerk and the intrigue of a Greek of the lower empire.

—Benjamin Disraeli, British
prime minister

PEEL, SIR ROBERT
1788-1850, British prime minister

Did you think, when, to serve your turn [as Prime Minister], you called the Devil up, that it was as easy to lay him as to raise him? Did you think, when you went on, session after session thwarting and reviling those whom you knew to be in the wrong, that the day of reckoning would never come? It has come. There you sit, doing penance for the disingenuousness of years.

—T.B. Macaulay, historian, statesman,
essayist, and poet

The right honourable gentleman's smile is like the silver fittings on a coffin.

—Benjamin Disraeli, British
prime minister

PITT, WILLIAM (THE YOUNGER), EARL OF CHATHAM

1759-1806, British prime minister

He was not merely a chip off the old block, but the old block itself.

—Edmund Burke, statesman
and orator

Lord Chatham commented about an approaching debate. "If I cannot speak standing, I will speak sitting, and if I cannot speak sitting, I will speak lying."

"Which he will do in whatever position he speaks," commented Lord North [Lord Frederick North, British prime minister].

✿ ✿ ✿

With death doomed to grapple
Beneath this cold slab, he
Who lied in the Chapel
Now lies in the Abbey.

—Lord Byron, poet

POINCARÉ, RAYMOND

1860-1934, French prime minister and president

This devil of a man is the opposite of Briand: The latter knows nothing, and understands everything; the other knows everything and understands nothing.

—Georges Clemenceau, French
president and statesman

RANDOLPH (OF ROANOKE), JOHN

1773-1833, politician and congressman from Virginia

Randolph was reputed to be impotent:
Sir, Divine Providence takes care of his own universe. Moral monsters cannot propagate. Impotent of everything but malevolence of purpose, they cannot otherwise multiply miseries than by blaspheming all that is pure and prosperous and happy. Could demon propagate demon, the universe might become a pandemonium; but I rejoice that the Father of Lies can never become the Father of Liars. One adversary of God and man is enough for one universe.

—Tristam Burges, congressman
from Rhode Island

REAGAN, RONALD

1911-   , actor, governor, presidential candidate

He's a nice man. He's a great elder statesman in this [Republican] party.

—John R. Connally, during the 1979
U.S. presidential primary campaign

ROCKEFELLER, NELSON A.

1908-1979, U.S. vice-president

Where was old Nels [Nelson] when you and I were dodging bullets in the Solomon Islands?

—John F. Kennedy, U.S. president,
addressing journalist
Benjamin C. Bradlee

ROCKINGHAM, MARQUIS OF (CHARLES WATSON WENTWORTH)

1730-1782, British prime minister

He could neither speak nor write with ease, and was handicapped by inexperience, boils, and a passion for Newmarket.

—O.A. Sherard, author

RUSSELL, JOHN , FIRST EARL

1792-1878, British prime minister

If a traveller were informed that such a man was leader of the House of Commons, he may begin to comprehend how the Egyptians worshipped an Insect. You are now exhaling upon the constitution of your country all that long-hoarded venom and all those distempered humours that have for years accumulated in your petty heart and tainted the current of your mortified life.

—Benjamin Disraeli, British
prime-minister

You say you are not convinced by my pamphlet. I am afraid that I am a very arrogant person, but I do assure you, that in the fondest moments of self-conceit, the idea of convincing a Russell that he was wrong never came across my mind. Euclid would have had a bad chance with you if you had happened to have formed an opinion that the interior angles of a triangle were not equal to two right angles. The more poor Euclid demonstrated, the more you would have not have been convinced.

—Sidney Smith, clergyman and essayist

SALISBURY, THIRD MARQUIS OF (ROBERT ARTHUR TALBOT GASCOYNE CECIL)

1830-1903, British prime minister

... that strange powerful inscrutable and brilliant obstructive deadweight at the top.

—Lord George Curzon, statesman

I am always very glad when Lord Salisbury makes a great speech ... It is sure to contain at least one blazing indiscretion which is a delight to remember.

—A.E. Parker, Earl of
Morley, statesman

His face is livid, gaunt his white body, his breath is green with gall; his tongue drips poison.

—John Quincy Adams, U.S. president

SEWARD, WILLIAM HENRY

1801-1872, politician

... a dirty abolitionist sneak.

—Mary Todd Lincoln, wife
of the president

SHAFTESBURY, FIRST EARL OF (ANTHONY ASHLEY COOPER)

1621-1683, statesman

A little limping peer—though crazy yet in action nimble and as busy as a body-louse.

—Anonymous

SHAFTESBURY, SEVENTH EARL OF (ANTHONY ASHLEY COOPER)

1801-1885, philanthropist, statesman

Lord Shaftesbury would have been in a lunatic asylum if he had not devoted himself to reforming lunatic asylums.
—Florence Nightingale, founder of modern nursing

SHERIDAN, RICHARD BRINSLEY

1751-1816, statesman, dramatist

Every man has his element: Sheridan's is hot water.
—Lord John Eldon, statesman and jurist

Fox outlived his vices; those of Sheridan accompanied him to the tomb.
—Sir Nathaniel Wraxall, author

SIMON, JOHN ALLESBROOK, VISCOUNT

1873-1954, British foreign secretary

Simon has sat on the fence so long that the iron has entered his soul.
—David Lloyd George, British prime minister

SMITH, ALFRED EMANUEL

1873-1944, governor, presidential candidate

The plain fact is that Al, as a good New Yorker, is as provincial as a Kansas farmer. He is not only not interested in the great problems that heave and lather the country; he has never heard of them.

—H.L. Mencken, writer,
editor, and critic

STEPHENS, ALEXANDER HAMILTON

1812-1883, politician

Never have I seen so small a nubbin come out of so much husk.

—Abraham Lincoln, U.S president

STEVENS, THADDEUS

1792-1868, politician, lawyer

His mind, as far as his sense of obligation to God was concerned, was a howling wilderness.

—Jeremiah Black, American cabinet officer

STEVENS, ADLAI EWING

1900-65, statesman, diplomat, lawyer

The real trouble with Stevenson is that he's no better than a regular sissy.

—Harry S Truman, U.S. president

Adlai Stevenson was a man who could never make up his mind whether he had to go to the bathroom or not.

—Harry S Truman

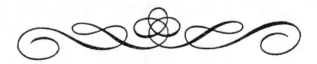

SUMNER, CHARLES
1811-1874, U.S. senator, abolitionist

... the most completely nothin' of a man that ever crossed my threshold,—naught whatsoever in him or of him but wind and vanity.

> —Thomas Carlyle, Scottish historian,
> philosopher, and essayist

He works his adjectives so hard that if they ever catch him alone, they will murder him.

> —Edwin L. Godkin, American editor

A foul-mouthed poltroon, [who] when caned for cowardly vituperation falls to the floor in an inanimate lump of incarnate cowardice.

> —Anonymous

TAFT, ROBERT ALPHONSO
1889-1953, politician

... He has a positive genius for being wrong. He is an authentic living representative of the old Bourbons of whom it was said that they "learned nothing, forgot nothing."

> —Marvin Harrison, author
> of *Robert A. Taft, Our*
> *Illustrious Dunderhead*

TILDEN, SAMUEL JONES
1814-1886, politician

Mr. Tilden is incapable of doing the simplest thing without a mask.

> —Anonymous

TRUDEAU, PIERRE ELLIOTT

1919-   , Canadian prime minister

In Pierre Elliott Trudeau Canada has at last produced a political leader worthy of assassination.

—Irving Layton, author and poet

TWEED, WILLIAM MARCY

1823-1878, politician

His nose is half-Brougham, half-Roman, and a man with a nose of that sort is not a man to be trifled with.

—Francis G. Fairfield, author

Mr. Tweed is inspired to all high and noble aims, by the contemplation of personal beauty and innocence as imbedded in a photograph of himself.

—Anonymous

WALLACE, GEORGE C.

1919-   , governor of Alabama and presidential candidate

1938—Hitler-Goering, 1968—Wallace-LeMay
If you liked Hitler, You'll Love Wallace.
Wallace über alles.

—Anti-Wallace campaign barbs

WALLACE, HENRY AGARD

1888-1965, U.S. vice-president

Henry Wallace was a fellow who wanted to be a great man, but didn't know how to go about it.

—Harry S Truman, U.S. president

Much of what Mr. Wallace calls his global thinking is, no matter how you slice it, still Globaloney.

—Clare Booth Luce, playwright
and diplomat

I have never been more disappointed in a public official. He was a muddled, totally irrational man, almost incapable of uttering a coherent sentence. He was also the bitterest man I have ever encountered.

—Harry S Truman, U.S. president

WALPOLE, SIR ROBERT, FIRST EARL OF ORFORD

1676-1745, British prime minister

Profuse and appetent, his ambition was subservient to his desire of making a great fortune. He had more of the Mazarin than of the Richelieu. He would do mean things for profit, and never thought of doing great ones for glory.

—Lord Chesterfield, statesman and author

WEBSTER, DANIEL

1782-1852, statesman, orator, and politician

The word liberty in the mouth of Mr. Webster sounds like the word love in the mouth of a courtesan.

—Ralph Waldo Emerson, poet

... The most meanly and foolishly treacherous man I ever heard of.

—James Russell Lowell, poet

. . . The gigantic intellect, the envious tempers, the ravenous ambition, and the rotten heart of Daniel Webster.

—Daniel Quincy Adams, American
physician and educator

The word "honor" in the mouth of Mr. Webster is like the word "love" in the mouth of a whore.

—Ralph Waldo Emerson, poet

WELLES, GIDEON

1802-1878, politician

Welles is the most garrulous old woman you were ever annoyed by.

—George B. McClellan, Civil War general

Retire, O Gideon, to an onion farm
Ply any trade that's innocent and slow
Do anything, where you can do no harm
Go anywhere you fancy—only go.

—Anonymous

WILLKIE, WENDELL LEWIS

1892-1944, industrialist, political leader, and Republican
standard bearer

. . . a simple barefoot Wall Street lawyer.

—Harold Ickes, U.S. secretary
of the interior

Chapter Three

. . . .

ROYALTY
AND NOBILITY

In the age of emperors, kings, and other crowned rulers, the crime of *lèse-majesté* was among the most serious. The promise of certain imprisonment, and worse, kept in check the wittiest minds and sharpest tongues. Yet among the courtiers every public and private fault of the ruler was known, and sooner or later the royal failings reached the masses. The people composed ditties, other types of short verse, and related anecdotes at the expense of royalty.

But the great wits of the age could voice their opinions only in guarded letters to their closest and most dependable friends. These letters were "discovered" long after their writers were in the grave, well beyond royal reach. Other insults reported below represent the judgments of men forced into exile or preferring exile to serving detested royal masters. Some of the affronts merely convey the judgments of later generations.

ANNE

1665-1714, queen of England

I have tried here to render comprehensible some of the Inarticulates of this world by setting down my own reading of that Queen of Inarticulates—Anne Stuart.

—Beatrice Curtis Brown, author

Her friendships were flames to extravagant passion ending in aversion.

—Sarah Churchill, author

Anne . . .when in good humour, was meekly stupid, and when in bad humour, was sulkily stupid.

—T. B. Macaulay, historian

CHARLES II

1630-1685, king of England

Here lies our mutton-loving King
Whose word no man relies on.
Who never said a foolish thing,
And never did a wise one.

—The Earl of Rochester, English
poet and courtier

CHARLOTTE SOPHIA

1744-1818, queen consort to George III of England

Yes, I do think that the *bloom* of her ugliness is going off.

—Colonel Disbrowe (her chamberlain), in William Timbs's
A Century of Anecdote

GRAFTON, AUGUSTUS HENRY FITZROY, 3RD DUKE OF
1735-1811

Charles the First lived and died a hypocrite. Charles the Second was a hypocrite of another sort, and should have died upon the same scaffold. At the distance of a century, we see their different characters happily revived, and blended in your Grace. Sullen and severe without religion, profligate without gayety, you live like Charles the Second, without being an amiable companion, and, for aught I know, may die as his father did, without the reputation of a martyr.

—*The Letters of Junius* (whose anonymity has been preserved), 1769-1772

ELIZABETH I
1533-1603, queen of England

O dearest Bess
I like your dress;
Oh sweet Liz
I like your phiz;
Oh dearest Queen
I've never seen
A face more like
a soup-tureen.

—Anonymous in Arnold Silcock, *Verse and Worse*

An element of lovemaking in diplomacy was always very much to her taste.

—Conyers Read, author

A deep instinct made it almost impossible for her to come to a fixed determination upon any subject whatever. Or, if she did, she immediately proceeded to contradict her resolution with the utmost violence, and, after that, to contradict her contradiction more violenty still.

—Lytton Strachey, author

ETHELRED THE UNREADY
968?-1016, king of England

The career of his life is said to have been cruel in the beginning, wretched in the middle, and disgraceful in the end.

—William of Malmesbury, historian

THE FIRST FOUR GEORGES

I sing the Georges Four,
For Providence could stand no more.
Some say that far the worst
Of all the Four was George the First.
But yet by some 'tis reckoned
That worser still was George the second.
And what mortal ever heard?
And good of George the Third?
When George the Fourth from earth descended
Thank God the line of Georges ended.

—Walter Savage Landor, author

GEORGE I

1660-1727, king of England

George the First knew nothing and desired to know nothing; did nothing and desired to do nothing; and the only good thing that is told of him is that he wished to restore the crown to its hereditary successor.

—Samuel Johnson, in James
Boswell's *Life of Johnson*

George I kept his wife in prison because he believed that she was no better than he was.

—Will Cuppy, author

A dull, stupid and profligate King, full of drink and low conversation, without dignity of appearance or manner, without sympathy of any kind with the English people and English ways, and without the slightest knowledge of the English language.

—Justin McCarthy, in Lewis
Melville's *The First George*

GEORGE II

1683-1760, king of England

The best, perhaps, that can be said of him is that on the whole, all things considered, he might have been worse.

—Justiin McCarthy

GEORGE III
1738-1820, king of England

> George the Third
> Ought never to have occurred.
> One can only wonder
> At so grotesque a blunder.
>
> —E. Clerihew Bentley, poet

His maxims, in mid-career, were those of a conscientious bull in a china shop.

—Richard Pares, author

If he is to be blamed, it must not be for what he did, but for what he was—an unbalanced man of low intelligence. And if he is to be praised, it is because he attempted to discharge honourably tasks that were beyond his powers.

—J.H. Plumb, author

Throughout the greater part of his life George III was a kind of consecrated obstruction.

—Walter Bagehot, author

GEORGE IV
1762-1830, king of England

A more contemptible, cowardly, selfish, unfeeling dog does not exist than this king . . . with vices and weaknesses of the lowest and most contemptible order.

—Charles Greville, diarist

A corpulent Adonis of fifty.

—Leigh Hunt, poet

How Monarchs die is easily explain'd
And thus it might upon the Tomb be chisell'd,
As long as George the Fourth could reign
he reign'd,
And then he mizzled.

—Thomas Hood, author

A noble, hasty race he ran,
Superbly filthy and fastidious;
He was the world's first gentleman,
And made the appellation hideous,

—W.M. Praed, author of
proposed epitaph, 1825

HENRY VIII

1491-1547, king of England

. . . a pig, an ass, a dunghill, the spawn of an adder, a basilisk, a lying buffoon, a mad fool with a frothy mouth . . . a bubberly ass . . .

—Martin Luther, theologian
and religious reformer

Henry VIII perhaps approached as nearly to the ideal standard of perfect wickedness as the infirmities of human nature will allow.

—Sir James Mackintosh, author

The plain truth is, that he was a most intolerable ruffian, a disgrace to human nature, and a blot of blood and grease upon the History of England.

—Charles Dickens, author

JAMES II
1633-1701, king of England

Under the morose face there seemed to be a heart of stone.

—Alexander Smellie, author

MARY I (BLOODY MARY)
1516-1558, queen of England

Cursed Jezebel of England!

—John Knox, religious reformer

MARY STUART, QUEEN OF SCOTS
1542-1587

. . . the most notorious whore in all the world.

—Peter Wentworth, in J.E.
Neale's *Peter Wentworth*

NAPOLEON I (NAPOLEON BONAPARTE)
1769-1821, emperor of France

He is a great unrecognized incapacity.

—Carl Otto, prince of Bismarck

And now we come to one of the most illuminating figures in modern history, the figure of an adventurer and a wrecker, whose story seems to display with an extraordinary vividness the universal subtle conflict of egotism, vanity and personality . . . this dark little archaic personage, hard, compact, capable, unscrupulous, imitative, and neatly vulgar.

—H.G. Wells, author

NAPOLEON III

1808-1873, emperor of France

His mind was a kind of extinct sulphur-pit.

—Thomas Carlyle, author

SHAH OF IRAN (MOHAMMED REZA PAHLAVI)

1919-   , deposed king of Iran

So intransigent, so harsh, maybe even ruthless behind that sad face.

—Oriana Fallaci, journalist

He [Hassan of Morocco] and the Shah, both of them playboys at one time, are so serious now that they are kings. They must be overcompensating.

—John F. Kennedy, U.S. president

VICTORIA

1819-1901, queen of Great Britain and Ireland and empress of India

Nowadays, a parlour-maid as ignorant as Queen Victoria was when she came to the throne would be classed as mentally defective.

—Bernard Shaw, author

She's more of a man than I expected.

—Henry James, novelist
and critic

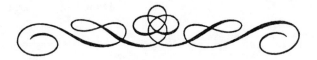

WILLIAM I (THE CONQUEROR)
1027-1087, king of England

William, indeed, seems to have been astute without wisdom, resolute without foresight, powerful without ultimate purpose, a man of very limited aims and very limited vision, narrow, ignorant and superstitious.

—R.G. Richardson and G.O.
Sayles, authors

WILLIAM III
1650-1702, king of England

A blockish damned Dutch mien, a hawkish beak,
With timorous eyes, who grunts when he should
speak.
Breathless and faint, he moves, or rather stumbles
Silent and dull he sits, and snorts or grumbles.

—Anonymous, *circa* 1688

WILLIAM IV
1754-1837, king of England

The King blew his nose twice, and wiped the royal perspiration repeatedly from a face which is probably the largest uncivilized spot in England.

—Oliver Wendell Holmes, author

They gave William IV a lovely funeral. It took six men to carry the beer.

—Louis Untermeyer, author

Chapter Four

• • • •

MEN AND WOMEN
OF LETTERS

In the realm of letters, slurs and other insulting remarks have been as common as in politics. Yet they need to be explained on different grounds.

In politics the "put-down" has often had a practical goal: to discredit an opponent or his progam and thereby win an election or put through one's own program. In literature, journalism, and criticism, a practical purpose may also be present, but it cannot account for the mass of insults flung at some writers. Nor can the many feuds, always fashionable in the literary world, provide a satisfactory explanation. Could it be that the creative ego, easily bruised, can keep itself intact only through verbal counterpunches? Writers have taken it on the chin not only from critics but even more often from fellow artists who were secretly or openly competing with them. Their skill with words and knowledge of character combine to produce the deadliest of affronts.

ADAMS, ABIGAIL

1744-1818, letter-writer, wife of President John Adams

The central and conspicuous fact about Abigail Adams's letters is that she hardly knew how to write a full paragraph.

—L.H. Butterfield, author

ADAMS, HENRY BROOKS

1838-1918, historian

. . . with the winds of a beautiful but ineffectual conscience beating vainly in a vacuum jar.

—T.S. Eliot, author

Henry Adams, snob, scholar, and misanthrope.

—Alfred Kazin, author

I want to look like an American Voltaire or Gibbon, but am slowly settling down to be a third-rate Boswell hunting for a Dr. Johnson.

—On himself

AKENSIDE, MARK

1721-1770, poet

I see they have published a splendid edition of Akensides' works. One bad Ode may be suffered, but a number of them together makes one sick.

—Samuel Johnson, writer, critic, and lexicographer

ALCOTT, LOUISA MAY

1832-1888, author

Living almost always among intellectuals, she preserved to the age of fifty-six that contempt for ideas which is normal among boys and girls of fifteen.

—Odell Shepard, poet

ALGER, HORATIO

1834-1899, author

Horatio Alger wrote the same novel 135 times and never lost his audience.

—George Juergens, author

ANDERSON, JACK NORMAN

1922-   , journalist

Jack Anderson is the lowest form of human being to walk the earth. He's a muckraker who lies, steals, and let me tell you this, Mr. [John] Dean, he'll go lower than dog shit for a story.

—J. Edgar Hoover, F.B.I. director

ANONYMOUS AUTHOR

On his two-line poem:

Very nice, though there are dull stretches.

—Antoine de Rivarol, author

From the moment I picked your book up until I laid it down I was convulsed with laughter. Some day I intend reading it.

—Groucho Marx, comedian

You may have genius. The contrary is, of course, probable.

—Oliver Wendell Holmes, U.S. Supreme Court Justice

ARETINO, PIETRO

1492-1556, Italian satirist

Here lies Aretino, Tuscan poet
Who spoke evil of everyone but God,
Giving the excuse "I never knew Him."

—Anonymous

The scourge of princes.

—Lodovico Ariosto, Italian poet

ARNOLD, MATTHEW

1822-1888, poet, critic

[Wordsworth's] Immortality Ode . . . is no more than moderately good . . . I put by its side the poems of Matthew Arnold, and think what a delightfully loud splash the two would make if I dropped them into a river.

—Dylan Thomas, poet

Poor Matt, he's gone to Heaven, no doubt—but he won't like God.

—Robert Louis Stevenson, author

AUDEN, WYSTAN HUGH
1907-1973, poet

A face like a wedding cake left out in the rain.

—Anonymous

. . . an engaging, bookish, American talent, too verbose to be memorable and too intellectual to be moving.

—Philip Larkin, English poet

Mr. Auden's brand of amoralism is only possible if you are the kind of person who is always somewhere else when the trigger is pulled.

—George Orwell, British
novelist and essayist

BARLOW, JOEL
1754-1812, poet, statesman

No poet with so little of poetry ever received so much of glory.

—Fred Lewis Pattee, authhor

BARRIE, SIR JAMES MATTHEW
1860-1937, playwright, novelist

Barrie struck twelve once—with *Peter Pan*—a subtly unwholesome sweetmeat, like most of his books.

—Florence Becker Lennon, author

Mr. Barrie is a born storyteller; and he sees no further than his stories—conceives any discrepancy between them and the world as a shortcoming on the world's part, and is only too happy to be able to rearrange matters in a pleasanter way.

—George Bernard Shaw, dramatist

BEAUMONT, FRANCIS
1584-1616, dramatist

The blossoms of Beaumont and Fletcher's imagination draw no sustenance from the soil, but are cut and slightly withered flowers stuck into sand. . .

—T.S. Eliot, poet

I confess to a condescending tolerance for Beaumont and Fletcher . . . The pair wrote a good deal that was pretty disgraceful; but at all events they had been educated out of the possibility of writing Titus Andronicus.

—George Bernard Shaw, dramatist

BEAVERBROOK, LORD
(WILLIAM MAXWELL AITKEN)
1879-1964, newspaper magnate

Beaverbrook is so pleased to be in the Government that he is like the town tart who has finally married the Mayor!

—Beverley Baxter

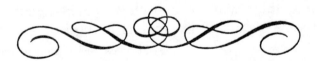

If Max gets to Heaven he won't last long. He will be chucked out for trying to pull off a merger between Heaven and Hell . . . after having secured a controlling interest in key subsidiary companies in both places, of course.

—H.G. Wells, English novelist,
historian, and socialist

BEERBOHM, SIR HENRY MAXIMILLIAN (MAX)
1872-1956, author, cartoonist

He has the most remarkable and seductive genius—and I should say about the smallest in the world.

—Lytton Strachey, English
biographer and critic

I was a modest, good-humoured boy. It is Oxford that has made me insufferable.

—On himself

The gods bestowed on Max the gift of perpetual old age.

—Oscar Wilde, British poet,
novelist, and dramatist

Tell me, when you are alone with Max, does he take off his face and reveal his mask?

—Oscar Wilde

BELLOC, JOSEPH HILAIRE PIERRE RENÉ
1870-1953, author, historian

Poor Mr. Belloc looked as though the grave were the only place for him.

—Evelyn Waugh, author

BENNETT, ENOCH ARNOLD
1867-1931, novelist

Bennett—sort of a pig in clover.

—D.H. Lawrence, author

The Hitler of the book-racket.

—Percy Wyndham Lewis, English
author and painter

BIERCE, AMBROSE GWINETT
1842-1914, journalist, author

He made a business of cracking skulls and ideas. Product of three disillusioning experiences, pioneer life, war, and journalistic uproars, he ended up with almost nothing that he could regard as sacred. He was an all-inclusive cynic.

—C. Hartley Grattan, author

Bierce would bury his best friend with a sigh of relief, and express satisfaction that he was done with him.

—Jack London, author

But there was no more discretion in Bierce than you will find in a runaway locomotive.

—H.L. Mencken, writer,
editor, and critic

BIRD, ROBERT MONTGOMERY
1806-1854, playwright, author

He had so many irons in the fire that he was never able to forge any single one into a weapon with which to conquer his world.

—Curtis Dahl, author

BLAKE, WILLIAM
1757-1827, poet, artist

He has no sense of the ludicrous, and, as to God, a worm crawling in a privy is as worthy an object as any other, as being to him indifferent. So to Blake the Chimney Sweeper etc. He is ruined by vain struggles to get rid of what presses on his brain—he attempts impossibles.

—William Hazlitt, English
essayist and critic

Be a god, your spirit cried;
Tread with feet that burn the dew;
Dress with clouds your locks of pride;
Be a child, God said to you.

—Oliver Dargan, author

BOSWELL, JAMES
1740-1795, author

You have but two topics, yourself and me, and I'm sick of both.

—Samuel Johnson, writer, critic,
and lexicographer

Boswell is a very clubable man.

—Samuel Johnson

It would be difficult to find a more shattering refutation of the lessons of cheap morality than the life of James Boswell. One of the most extraordinary successes in the history of civilization was achieved by an idler, a lecher, a drunkard, and a snob.

—Lytton Strachey, English
biographer and critic

Servile and impertinent, shallow and pedantic, a bigot and a sot, bloated with family pride, and eternally blustering about the dignity of a born gentleman, yet stooping to be a talebearer, and eavesdropper, a common butt in the taverns of London .. Everything which another man would have hidden, everything the publication of which would have made another man hang himself, was matter of exaltation to his weak and diseased mind.

—Thomas Babington Macaulay,
English historian, essayist,
poet, and statesman

Have you got Boswell's most absurd enormous book? The best thing in it is a *bon mot* of Lord Pembroke. The more one learns of Johnson, the more preposterous assemblage he appears of strong sense, of the lowest bigotry and prejudices, of pride, brutality, fretfulness and vanity—annd Boswell is the ape of most of his faults, without a grain of his sense. It it the story of a mountebank and his zany.

—Horace Walpole, British author

BOTTOMLEY, HORATIO WILLIAM

1860-1933, journalist, financier

England's Greatest Living Humbug.

—Reuben Bigland, author

He had two brains, that man. One linked up with his tongue and the other thought while he talked.

—Sir Harry Preston, author

BOURNE, RANDOLPH SILLIMAN

1886-1918, author, journalist

Never being competent to direct and manage any of the affairs of the world myself, I will be forced to set off by myself in the wilderness, howling like a coyote that everything is being run wrong.

—On himself

BROUN, HEYWOOD CAMPBELL

1888-1939, journalist

No one is so impotent that, meeting Broun face to face, he cannnot frighten him into any lie. Any mouse can make this elephant squeal.

—Alexander Woollcott, writer and critic

A gin-drinking, poker-playing, wicked old reprobate.

—Herbert B. Swope, journalist
and public official

Heywood Broun and I had one thing in common: he was fired from as many newspapers as I have been fired out of political parties.

—Fiorello La Guardia, mayor
of New York City

BROWNING, ROBERT
1812-1889, poet

He has plenty of music in him, but he cannot get it out.

—Alfred, Lord Tennyson, poet

The nearest he got to poetry was . . . Mrs. Browning. . . . His muse was as much invalid as his wife was invalide.

—Oliver St. J. Gogarty, author

BURKE, EDMUND
1729-1797, author, statesman

As he rose like a rocket, he fell like a stick.

—Thomas Paine, American Revolutionary writer and political thinker

Is he like Burke, who winds into a subject like a serpent?

—Oliver Goldsmith, British poet,
playwright, and novelist

He lived like a king, a despot in the realm of words.

—Desmond MacCarthy, author

BUTLER, SAMUEL
1835-1902, author

I am the enfant terrible of literature and science. If I cannot, and I know I cannot, get the literary and scientific bigwigs to give me a shilling, I can, and I know I can, heave bricks into the middle of them.

—On himself

BYRON, GEORGE GORDON NOEL, LORD
1788-1824, poet

Of all remembered poets the most wanting in distinction of any kind, the most dependent for his effects on the most violent and vulgar resources of rant and cant and glare and splash and splutter.

—Algernon Charles Swinburne,
English poet and critic

The most affected of sensualists and the most pretentious of profligates.

—Algernon Charles Swinburne

A denaturalized being who having exhausted every species of sensual gratification, and drained the cup of sin to its bitterest dregs, is resolved to show that he is no longer human, even in his frailties, but a cool, unconcerned fiend.

—John Styles

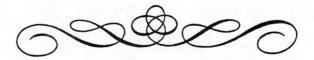

From the poetry of Lord Byron they drew a system of thics, compounded of misanthropy and voluptuousness, in which the two great commandments were, to hate your neighbour, and to love your neighbour's wife.

—T.B.Macaulay, British historian,
poet essayist, and statesman

He had a head which statuaries loved to copy, and a foot the deformity of which the beggars in the street mimicked.

—T.B. Macaulay

I hate the whole race of them, there never existed a more worthless set than Byron and his friends.

—Duke of Wellington, British
general and statesman

Ah, what a poet Bryon would have been had he taken his meals properly, and allowed himself to grow fat—and not have physicked his intellect with wretched opium pills and acrid vinegar, that sent his principles to sleep, and turned his feelings sour! If that man had respected his dinner, he never would have written Don Juan.

—W.M. Thackeray, author

The fact is, that first, the Italian women with whom he associates are perhaps the most contemptible of all who exist under the moon—the most ignorant, the most disgusting, the most bigoted; countesses smell so strongly of garlic, that an ordinary Englishman cannot approach them. Well, L.B. is familiar with the lowest sort of these women, the people his gondolieri pick up in the streets.

—Percy Bysshe Shelley, poet

So we have lost another poet. I never much relished his Lordship's mind, and shall be sorry if the Greeks have cause to miss him. He was to me offensive, and I can never make out his great power, which his admirers talk of. Why a line of Wordsworth's is a lever to lift the immortal spirit! Byron can only bore the Spleen. He was at best a Satyrist,—in any other way he was mean enough. I dare say I do him injustice; but I cannot love him, nor squeeze a tear to his memory.

—Charles Lamb, British essayist,
poet, and critic

Mad, bad, and dangerous to know.

—Lady Caroline Lamb, socialite
and Byron's lover

Lord Byron is the spoiled child of fame as well as fortune. He has taken a surfeit of popularity, and is not contented to delight, unless he can shock the public. He would force them to admire in spite of decency and common sense.

—William Hazlitt, British
essayist and critic

Of Byron one can say, as of no other English poet of his eminence, that he added nothing to the language, that he discovered nothing in the sounds, and developed nothing in the meaning, of individual words. I cannot think of any other poet of his distinction who might so easily have been an accomplished foreigner writing English.

—T.S. Eliot, poet

He seems to me the most vulgar-minded genius that ever produced a great effect in literature.

—George Eliot, British novelist

The world is rid of Lord Byron, but the deadly slime of his touch still remains.

—John Constable, British
landscape painter

Byron!—he would be all forgotten today if he had lived to be a florid old gentleman with iron-grey whiskers, writing very long, very able letters to *The Times* about the Repeal of the Corn Laws.

—Max Beerbohm, author
and caricaturist

> And poor, proud Byron, sad as grave
> And salt as life; forlornly brave,
> And quivering with the dart he gave.

—Elizabeth Barrett Browning, poet

So long as Byron tried to write Poetry with a capital P, to express deep emotions and profound thoughts, his work deserved that epithet he most dreaded, una seccatura. As a thinker he was, as Goethe perceived, childish, and he possessed neither the imaginative vision—he could never invent anything, only remember—nor the verbal sensibility such poetry demands.

—W.H. Auden, poet

CARLYLE, THOMAS, AND WIFE
1795-1881, historian and essayist

That very sorry pair of phenomena, Thomas Cloacina and his Goody.

—Algernon Charles Swinburne,
British poet and critic

It was very good of God to let Carlyle and Mrs. Carlyle marry one another and so make only two people miserable instead of four.

—Samuel Butler, novelist

Carlyle has led us all out into the desert, and he has left us there.

—A.H. Clough, British poet and educator

The same old sausage, fizzing and sputtering in its own grease.

—Henry James, American novelist
and essayist in England

CHESTERTON, GILBERT KEITH

1874-1936, novelist, poet, critic

Chesterton is like a vile scum on a pond . . . All his slop— it is really modern catholicism to a great extent, the *never* taking a hedge straight, the mumbojumbo of superstition dodging behind clumsy fun and paradox . . . I believe he creates a millieu in which art is impossible. He and his kind.

—Ezra Pound, poet

Chesterton's resolute conviviality is about as genial as an *auto dé fe* of teetotallers.

—George Bernard Shaw, dramatist

CHURCHILL, CHARLES

1731-1764, poet

Nay, Sir, I am a very fair judge. He did not attack me violently till he found I did not like his poetry; and his attack on me shall not prevent me from continuing to say what I think of him, from an apprehension that it may be ascribed to resentment. No, Sir, I called the fellow a blockhead at first, and I will call him a blockhead still.

—Samuel Johnson, writer, critic,
and lexicographer

COLERIDGE, SAMUEL TAYLOR
1772-1834, poet and critic

A weak, diffusive, weltering, ineffectual man . . . Never did I see such apparatus got ready for thinking, and so little thought. He mounts scaffolding, pulleys and tackle, gathers all the tools in the neighbourhood with labour, with noises, demonstration, precept, abuse, and sets—three bricks.

—Thomas Carlyle, historian
and essayist

"Did you ever hear me preach?" asked Samuel T. Coleridge.

"I never heard you do anything else," answered Charles Lamb.

—Charles Lamb, British essayist
poet, and critic

COLLINS, CHURTON
1848-1908, critic

A louse in the locks of literature.

—Alfred Lord Tennyson, poet

COMSTOCK, ANTHONY

1844-1915, American censor

Comstockery is the world's standing joke at the expense of the U.S. It confirms the deep-seated conviction of the Old World that America is a provincial place, a second-rate country town.

—George Bernard Shaw, author

Anthony Comstock may have been entirely correct in his assumption that the division of living creatures into male and female was a vulgar mistake, but a conspiracy of silence about the matter will hardly alter the facts.

—Heywood Broun, journalist

DE VOTO, BERNARD AUGUSTINE

1897-1955, American writer and editor

I denounce Mr. Bernard De Voto as a fool and a tedious and egotistical fool, as a liar and a pompous and boresome liar.

—Sinclair Lewis, novelist

DONNE, JOHN

1573-1631, poet, dean of St. Paul's

Dr. Donne's verses are like the peace of God; they pass all understanding.

—King James I, saying recorded by

DREISER, THEODORE

1871-1945, author

His style is atrocious, his sentences are chaotic, his grammar and syntax faulty; he has no feeling for words, no sense of diction. His wordiness and his repetitions are unbearable, his cacophonies incredible.

—T.K. Whipple, author

DRYDEN, JOHN

1631-1700, poet

If Dryden's plays had been as good as their prefaces he would have been a dramatist indeed.

—Harley Granville Barker, writer

EARP, T.W.

(n.d.), critic

> I heard a little chicken chirp;
> My name is Thomas, Thomas Earp,
> And I can neither paint nor write,
> I can only put other people right.

—D.H. Lawrence, British novelist
and poet

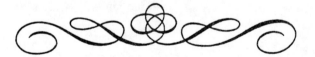

ELIOT, GEORGE (MARY ANN EVANS)
1819-1880, novelist

George Eliot had the heart of Sappho; but the face, with the long proboscis,, the protruding teeth of the Apocalyptic horse, betrayed animality.

—George Meredith, British
novelist and poet

I found out in the first two pages that it was a woman's writing—she supposed that in making a door, you last of all put in the *panels!*

—Thomas Carlyle, Scottish historian,
author, and essayist; after
reading *Adam Bede*

ELIOT, THOMAS STEARNS
1888-1965, poet

Mr. Eliot . . . is at times an excellent poet and . . . has arrived at the supreme Eminence among English critics largely through disguising himself as a corpse.

—Ezra Pound, American poet

That awful boresome man? You can't be serious! Why he's so *stoopid!* He's such a *bore*, don't you know? I have to tell him all the clues!

—Henry Bradshaw Isherwood, (on doing
crosswords with TSE in their club),
in Christopher Isherwood's *Kath-
leen and Frank*

EMERSON, RALPH WALDO

1803-1882, essayist, poet

One of the seven humbugs of Xtiandom.

—William Morris, English poet,
artist designer, social
reformer, and printer

[Emerson's words about Swinburne are] . . . the last tricks
of tongue now possible to a gap-toothed and hoary-headed
ape, . . who now in his dotage spits and chatters from a dir-
tier perch of his own finding and fouling: coryphaeus, or
choragus of his Bulgarian tribe of autocoprophagous
baboons.

—Algernon C. Swinburne,
British poet and critic

The critic Gosse inquired one day of A.C. Swinburne
whether he had taken further notice of the feud with Emerson. When told he had, Gosse expressed the hope that Swinburne's language was more moderate. "Perfectly moderate," Swinburne assured Gosse, "I merely informed him, in
language of the strictest reserve, that he was a hoary-headed
and toothless baboon, who, first lifted into notice on the
shoulder of Carlyle, now spits and splutters from a filthier
platform of his own finding and fouling. That is all I've
said."

—Algernon C. Swinburne

Like most poets, preachers, and metaphysicians, he burst
into conclusions at a spark of evidence.

—Henry Seidel Canby, author

Emerson is one who lives instinctively on ambrosia—and leaves everything indigestible on his plate.

—Friedrich Nietzsche, philosopher

I could readily see in Emerson a gaping flaw. It was the insinuation that had he lived in those days when the world was made, he might have offered some valuable suggestions.

—Herman Melville, novelist
and poet

There comes Emerson first, whose rich words,
    every one,
Are like gold nails in temples to hang trophies on;
Whose prose is grand verse, while his verse,
    the Lord knows,
Is some of it pr—No 'tis not even prose.

—James Russell Lowell, poet, essayist,
editor, and diplomat

ETHEREGE, SIR GEORGE
1634?-1691, English dramatist

Etherege writes *Airy Songs*, and soft Lampoons,
The best of any Man; as for your *Nouns*,
Grammar, and *Rules of Art*, he knows 'em not,
Yet writ two Talking *Plays* without one Plot.

—John Wilmot, Earl of Rochester,
poet and courtier

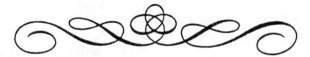

FERBER, EDNA

1887-1968, author

Miss Ferber, who was fond of wearing tailored suits, showed up at the Round Table one afternoon sporting a new suit similar to one Nöel Coward was wearing. "You look almost like a man," Coward said as he greeted her. "So," Miss Ferber replied, "do you."

—Robert E. Drennan, author

FIELDING, HENRY

1707-1754, novelist

Fielding had as much humour perhaps as Addison, but, having no idea of grace, is perpetually disgusting.

—Horace Walpole, Earl of
Orford, British writer

FITZGERALD, FRANCIS SCOTT KEY

1896-1940, author

In fact, Mr. Fitzgerald—I believe that is how he spells his name—seems to believe that plagiarism begins at home.

—Zelda Fitzgerald, his wife

FLEMING, IAN LANCASTER

1908-1964, novelist

Your descriptive passages, as usual, are very good indeed . . . I am willing to accept the centipede, the tarantulas, the land crabs, the giant squid . . . I am even willing to forgive your reckless use of invented verbs—"I inch, Thou inchest,

He snakes, I snake, We Palp, They palp", etc., but what I will neither accept nor forgive is the highly inaccurate statement that when it is eleven a.m. in Jamaica, it is six a.m. in dear old England. This, dear boy, to put not too fine a point on it, is a f— lie. When it is eleven a.m. in Jamaica, it is *four p.m.* in dear old England, and it is carelessness of this kind that makes my eyes slits of blue.

—Noel Coward, British playwright,
actor, and composer

The trouble with Ian is that he gets off with women because he can't get on with them.

—Rosamond Lehmann, British novelist

FORD, FORD MADOX (for HERMANN HUEFFER)
1873-1939, author

. . . His mind was like a Roquefort cheese, so ripe that it was palpably falling to pieces.

—Van Wyck Brooks, American critic

His forlorn attempts to throw a smoke-screen round himself produced through the distorted haze, the apparition of a monster, like a pink elephant, absurd, bizarre, immense.

—Edward Crankshaw

So fat and Buddhistic and nasal that a dear friend described him as an animated adenoid.

—Norman Douglas, British
novelist and essayist

Hueffer was a flabby lemon and pink giant, who hung his mouth open as though he were an animal at the Zoo inviting buns—especially when ladies were present. . .

—Percy Wyndham Lewis, British author and painter

Master, mammoth mumbler.

—Robert Lowell, poet

FORSTER, EDWARD MORGAN

1879-1970, novelist

He's a mediocre man—and knows it, or suspects it, which is worse; he will come to no good, and in the meantime he's treated rudely by waiters and is not really admired even by middle-class dowagers.

—Lytton Strachey, British biographer and critic

E.M. Forster never gets any further than warming the teapot. He's a rare fine hand at that. Feel this teapot. Is it not beautifully warm? Yes, but there ain't going to be no tea.

—Katherine Mansfield, British author

FROUDE, JAMES ANTHONY

1818-1894, historian

. . . a desultory and theoretical littérateur who wrote more rot on the reign of Elizabeth than Gibbon required for all the Decline and Fall . . .

—Algernon Turnor

. . . in Froudes' case the loss of his faith turned out to be rather like the loss of a heavy portmanteau, which one afterwards discovers to have been full of rags and brickbats.

—Lytton Strachey, British
biographer and critic

FULLER, (SARAH) MARGARET (MARCHIONESS OSSOLI)

1810-1850, transcendentalist, social reformer, critic

. . . to whom Venus gave everything except beauty, and Pallas everything except wisdom.

—Oscar Wilde, British poet,
novelist, and dramatist

She wrote so gracelessly and effusively, and sometimes with such lack of simple clarity, that reading her was anything but a pleasure even to her friends and neighbors.

—Bernard Smith, author

She was a great humbug; of course with much talent, and much moral ideality, or else she could not have been so great a humbug. But she had stuck herself full of borrowed qualities, which she chose to provide herself with, but which had not root in her.

—Nathaniel Hawthorne, author

GARRISON, WILLIAM LLOYD

1805-1879, American editor, lecturer, and abolitionist

William Lloyd Garrison is a tart Luther who neighs like a horse.

—Ralph Waldo Emerson, American
essayist, philosopher, and poet

GIBBON, EDWARD

1737-1794, historian

There is no Gibbon but Gibbon and Gibbon is his prophet. The solemn march of his cadences, the majestic impropriety of his innuendo are without rivals in the respective annals of British eloquence and British indelicacy.

—Philip Guedella, author

Gibbon's style is detestable; but it is not the worst thing about him.

—Samuel Taylor Coleridge,
British poet and critic

GILBERT, SIR WILLIAM SCHWENK

1836-1911, dramatist, lyricist

Another week's rehearsal with WSG & I should have gone raving mad. I had already ordered some straw for my hair.

—Sir Arthur Seymour Sullivan,
British composer

GOLDSMITH, OLIVER

1728-1774, poet, dramatist

It is amazing how little Goldsmith knows. He seldom comes where he is not more ignorant than anyone else.

—Samuel Johnson, British writer,
critic, and lexicographer

The misfortune of Goldsmith in conversation is this: he goes on without knowing how he is to get off.

—Samuel Johnson

Poor fellow! He hardly knew an ass from a mule, nor a turkey from a goose, but when he saw it on the table.

—Richard Cumberland, author

Here lies Nolly Goldsmith, for shortness called
   Noll,
Who wrote like an angel, and talk'd like poor Poll.

—David Garrick, actor

Goldsmith's mind was entirely unfurnished. When he was engaged in a work, he had all his knowledge to find, which when he found, he knew how to use, but forgot it immediately after he had used it.

—Sir Joshua Reynolds, British portrait painter

GRAY, THOMAS
1716-1771, poet

Sir, he was dull in company, dull in his closet, dull everywhere. He was dull in a new way, and that made many people think him GREAT. He was a mechanical poet.

—Samuel Johnson, English writer, critic, and lexicographer

I do not profess to be a person of very various reading; nevertheless, if I were to pluck out of Gray's tail all the feathers which I know belong to other birds, he would be left very bare indeed.

—William Wordsworth, British poet laureate

GREELEY, HORACE

1811-1872, editor, political leader

. . . poor Greeley . . . nincompoop without genius.

—James Gordon Bennett, Sr.,
American newspaper proprietor

GREGORY, ISABELLA AUGUSTA, LADY

1852-1932, author

Now that the Abbey Players are world-renowned, I begin
to realize that with such an audience and such actors an
author is hardly needed. Good acting covers a multitude of
defects. It explains the success of Lady Gregory's plays.

—Oliver St. J. Gogarty, author

GREVILLE, CHARLES CAVENDISH FULKE

1794-1865, diarist

He is the most conceited person with whom I have ever
been brought in contact, although I have read Cicero and
known Bulwer Lytton.

—Benjamin Disraeli, British
statesman and writer

GREY, ZANE

1875-1939, American novelist

You've wasted enough of our time with your junk. Why
don't you go back to filling teeth? You can't write, you never
could write, and you never will be able to write.

—a publisher

HARRIS, FRANK

1856-1931, author, journalist

In fact Frank Harris has no feelings. It is the secret of his success. Just as the fact that he thinks that other people have none either is the secret of failure that lies in wait for him somewhere on the way of Life.

—Oscar Wilde, British poet,
novelist, and dramatist

Frank Harris is invited to all the great houses in England —once.

—Oscar Wilde

HARTE, (FRANCIS) BRET

1836-1902, author

Harte, in a mild and colorless way, was that kind of man —that is to say, he was a man without a country; no, not a man—man is too strong a term; he was an invertebrate without a country.

—Mark Twain, American
novelist and humorist

He hadn't a sincere fiber in him. I think he was incapable of emotion for I think he had nothing to feel with.

—Mark Twain

HAWTHORNE, NATHANIEL

1804-1864, author

. . . he never seemed to be doing anything, and yet he did not like to be disturbed at it.

—John Greenleaf Whittier, poet

Nathaniel Hawthorne's reputation as a writer is a very pleasing fact, because his writing is not good for anything, and this is a tribute to the man.

—Ralph Waldo Emerson, American essayist, philosopher, and poet

HAZLITT, WILLIAM
1778-1830, essayist

Hazlitt .. had perhaps the most uninteresting mind of all our distinguished critics.

—T.S. Eliot, American poet, critic, and essayist

His manners are 99 in a 100 singularly repulsive.

—Samuel Taylor Coleridge, British poet and critic

This miscreant, Hazlitt, continues ... his abuse of Southey, Coleridge and myself in the "Examiner." I hope that you do not associate with the fellow; he is not a proper person to be admitted into respectable society, being the most perverse and malevolent creature that ill-luck has thrown my way. Avoid him. . .

—William Wordsworth, poet

. . . why could you tell Mr. Shelley in a pleasant manner of what you dislike in him? . . . How do you think that friends can eternally live upon their good behaviour in this way, and be cordial and comfortable or whatever else you choose they should be—for it is difficult to find out—on pain of being drawn and quartered in your paragraphs.

—Leigh Hunt, poet and littérateur

He abuses all poets, with the single exception of Milton; he abuses all country-people; he abuses the English; he abuses the Irish; he abuses the Scotch. . . . if the creature . . . must make his way over the tombs of illustrious men, disfiguring the records of their greatness with the slime and filth which marks his track, it is right to point him out, that he may be flung back to the situation in which nature designed that he should grovel.

—*Quarterly Review*, 1817

A mere ulcer; a sore from head to foot; a poor devil so completely flayed that there is not a square inch of healthy flesh on his carcass; an overgrown pimple, sore to the touch.

—*Quarterly Review*, 1817

HEARST, WILLIAM RANDOLPH

1863-1951, newspaper proprietor

He wrote so much about the Yellow Peril that his journalism took its distinctive coloration from the subject.

—Richard Armour, author

HEINE, HEINRICH

1797-1856, German poet

My head today is perfectly barren and you will find me stupid enough, for a friend has been here, and we exchanged ideas.

—On himself

HEMINGWAY, ERNEST MILLER
1899-1961, author

A literary style . . . of wearing false hair on the chest.

—Max Eastman, author

HERRICK, ROBERT
1591-1674, poet

Of all our poets this man appears to have had the coarsest mind. Without being intentionally obscene, he is thoroughly filthy, and has not the slightest sense of decency. In an old writer, and especially one of that age, I never saw so large a proportion of what may truly be called either trash or ordure.

—Robert Southey, British author

HERVEY OF ICKWORTH, JOHN HERVEY, BARON
1696-1743, British memoirist

Yet let me flap this bug with gilded wings,
This painted child of dirt, that stinks and stings.

—Alexander Pope, British poet

HILDRETH, RICHARD
1807-1865, historian, editor, lawyer

As venomous and deaf as an adder . . .

—Richard Henry Dana, American
poet and essayist

HOLMES, OLIVER WENDELL
1809-1894, essayist, poet, teacher

Not since Robert Treat Paine had there been such a master of Yankee small talk . . . But like every talker his discursiveness is inveterate; he wanders far in pursuit of his point and sometimes returns empty-handed. He was always an amateur; life was too agreeable for him to take the trouble to become an artist.

—Vernon Louis Parrington, author

Holmes was an aristocrat even to the extent of having a slight repugnance to people who smelled too much of mere literary pursuits.

—Alexander Cowie, author

HOPPER, HEDDA
1890-1966, journalist

Timid? As timid as a buzzsaw.

—Casey Shawhan

HOWELLS, WILLIAM DEAN
1837-1920, author

The truth about Howells is that he really has nothing to say, for all the charm he gets into saying it. His psychology is superficial, amateurish, often nonsensical; his irony is scarcely more than a polite facetiousness; his characters simply refuse to live.

—H.L. Mencken, American
writer, editor, and critic

HUME, PAUL

(n.d.), music critic of the Truman Era

I have just read your lousy review buried in the back pages. You sound like a frustrated old man who never made a success, an eight-ulcer on a four-ulcer job and all four ulcers working.

I never met you, but if I do you'll need a new nose and a supporter below. Westbrook Pegler, a guttersnipe, is a gentleman compared to you. You can take that as more of an insult than a reflection on your ancestry.

—Harry S Truman, U.S. president

Paul Hume didn't know a damn thing about music. Not a goddam thing. When he wrote about Margaret in the Washington *Post*, he showed he didn't know a thing about music. He was just a smart aleck and a showoff . . .

—Harry S Truman

HUXLEY, ALDOUS LEONARD

1894-1963, novelist

I don't like his books; even if I admire a sort of desperate courage of repulsion and repudiation in them. But again, I feel only half a man writes the books—a sort of precocious adolescent.

—D.H. Lawrence, British
novelist and poet

You were right about Huxley's book (*Ape and Essence*) —it is awful. And do you notice that the more holy he gets, the more his books stink with sex? He cannot get off the subject of flagellating women.

—George Orwell, British
novelist and essayist

You could always tell by his conversation which volume of the *Encyclopedia Britannica* he'd been reading. One day it would be Alps, Andes and Apennines, and the next it would be the Himalayas and the Hippocratic Oath.

—Bertrand Russell, British philosopher,
mathematician, and writer

JAMES, HENRY
1843-1916, novelist

It's not that he "bites off more than he can chew," as T.G. Appleton said of Nathan, but he chews more than he bites off.

—Mrs. Henry Adams, wife
of American historian

. . . For the first quarter of an hour of our conversation with him we are largely impressed with his variety, his catholicity; after that comes a certain indescribable sense of vagueness, of superficiality, of indifferentism; finally, if we must give the thing a name, a forlorn feeling of vacuity, of silliness.

—Robert Williams Buchanan,
British poet and novelist

Henry James was one of the nicest old ladies I ever met.

—William Faulkner, author

When he isn't being a great and magnificent author, he certainly can be a very fussy and tiresome one.

—Ezra Pound, American poet

JEFFREY, FRANCIS, LORD

1773-1850, critic and essayist

No one minds what Jeffrey says . . . It's not more than a week ago that I heard him speak disrespectfully of the Equator.

—Sydney Smith, clergyman and essayist

JOHNSON, SAMUEL (DOCTOR)

1709-1784, critic, poet, lexicographer

Dr. Johnson's sayings would not appear so extraordinary, were it not for his bow-wow way.

—Lord Pembroke (Henry Herbert),
author and literary patron

Johnson made the most brutal speeches to living persons; for though he was good-natured at bottom, he was ill-natured at top. He loved to dispute to show his superiority. If his opponents were weak, he told them they were fools; if they vanquished him, he was scurrilous.

—Horace Walpole, English writer

Upon Johnson's death:
Here lies Sam Johnson: —Reader, have a care,
Tread lightly, lest you wake a sleeping bear;
Religious, moral, generous and humane
He was; but self-sufficient, proud and vain.
Fond of, and overbearing in, dispute,
A Christian and a scholar—but a brute.

—Soame Jenkyns, poet

That pompous preacher of melancholy moralities.

—Jeremy Bentham, author

JONES, HENRY ARTHUR
1851-1929, British dramatist

The first rule for a young playwright to follow is not to write like Henry Arthur Jones. The second and third rules are the same.

—Oscar Wilde, British poet,
novelist and dramatist

JONSON, BENJAMIN
1573-1637, dramatist, poet

To know Ben Jonson was in Jonson's eyes a liberal profession.

—Charles Whibley, author

JOYCE, JAMES
1882-1941, Irish novelist

The work of a queasy undergraduate scratching his pimples.

—Virginia Woolf, novelist

The last part of it [*Ulysses*] is the dirtiest, most indecent, most obscene thing ever written. Yes, it is . . . it is filthy.

—D.H. Lawrence, novelist

It [*Ulysses*] is written by a man with a diseased mind and soul so black that he would even obscure the darkness of hell.

—a U.S. senator

I have difficulty in describing . . . the character of Mr. Joyce's morality . . . he is a literary charlatan of the extremest order . . . He is a sort of M. de Sade, but does not write so well.

—Edmund Gosse, British critic

KAUFMAN, GEORGE S.
1889-1961, playwright, journalist

He was like a dry cracker. Brittle.

—Edna Ferber, American
novelist and playwright

KEATS, JOHN
1795-1821, poet

A tadpole of the Lakes.

—Lord Byron, poet

The kind of man that Keats was gets ever more horrible to me. Force of hunger for pleasure of every kind, and want of all other force—such a soul, it would once have been very evident, was a chosen "vessel of Hell"; and truly, for ever there is justice in that feeling.

—Thomas Carlyle, Scottish historian,
philosopher, and essayist

KILGALLEN, DOROTHY

1913-1965, newspaper columnist

Dorothy Kilgallen is the only woman I wouldn't mind my wife catching me with . . . I don't know why she took such umbrage at my comments on birth control, she's such a living argument for it.

—Johnny Carson, U.S.
television personality

KILMER, JOYCE

1886-1918, American poet

"Trees" is one of the most annoying pieces of verse within my knowledge. Surely the Kilmer tongue must not have been very far from the Kilmer cheek when he wrote, "Poems are made by fools like me."

—Heywood Campbell Broun, American
newspaper columnist and critic

KIPLING, (JOSEPH) RUDYARD
1865-1936, author

Mr. Kipling . . . stands for everything in this cankered world which I would wish were otherwise.

—Dylan Thomas, Welsh poet

LAMB, CHARLES
1775-1834, British essayist and humorist

Charles Lamb I sincerely believe to be in some considerable degree insane. A more pitiful, rickety, gasping stammering Tomfool I do not know. He is witty by denying truisms and abjuring good manners. His speech wriggles hither and thither with an incessant painful fluctuation, not an opinion in it, or a fact, or a phrase that you can thank him for—more like a convulsion fit than a natural systole and diastole. Besides, he is now a confirmed, shameless drunkard; asks vehemently for gin and water in strangers' houses, tipples till he is utterly mad . . . Poor Lamb! Poor England! when such a despicable abortion is named genius!

—Thomas Carlyle, Scottish historian,
philosopher, and essayist

LANIER, SIDNEY
1842-1881, poet, musician, critic

If one reads very much of Lanier, one is tempted in the long run to lose patience with him. He is at once insipid and florid. He is noble, to be sure, but his nobility is boring; his eloquence comes to seem empty.

—Edmund Wilson, author

LAWRENCE, DAVID HERBERT
1885-1930, novelist, poet, painter, playwright

For Lawrence, existence was one continuous convalescence; it was as though he were newly re-born from a mortal illness every day of his life.

—Aldous Huxley, British novelist,
poet, and essayist

LAWRENCE, THOMAS EDWARD (OF ARABIA)
1888-1935, author, soldier

Arabian Lawrence, who, whatever his claims as a man, was surely a sonorous fake as a writer.

—Kingsley Amis, author

LEVANT, OSCAR
1906-1972, author, actor, musician

There is absolutely nothing wrong with Oscar Levant that a miracle cannot fix.

—Alexander Woollcott, American
writer and critic

LEWIS, PERCY WYNDHAM
1884-1957, novelist, painter

That lonely old volcano of the Right.

—W.H. Auden, English poet

I do not think I have ever seen a nastier-looking man . . . Under the black hat, when I had first seen them, the eyes had been those of an unsuccessful rapist.

—Ernest Hemingway, American
novelist and short-story writer

A buffalo in wolf's clothing.

—Robert Ross

LODGE, THOMAS
1558-1625, author

In wit, simple; in learning, ignorant; in attempt, rash; in name, Lodge.

—Stephen Gosson, author

LONDON, JACK
1876-1916, writer

. . . . easy to critcize him, easy to deplore him, impossible to avoid him.

—Fred Lewis Pattee, educator

Like Peter Pan, he never grew up, and he lived his own stories with such intensity that he ended by believing them himself.

—Ford Madox Ford, British author

LONGFELLOW, HENRY WADSWORTH
1807-1882, poet

His didactics are all out of place. He has written brilliant poems, by accident; that is to say, when permitting his genius to get the better of his conventional habit of thinking, a habit deduced from German study.

—Edgar Allan Poe, American poet,
critic, and fiction writer

LOWELL, AMY

1874-1925, poet, critic

Her bodily frame was excessively stout and ungainly; her face held something childish, self-consciously prim, and almost mediocre, with a sleek urbanity of self-assurance grown from her long cultural background.

—Clement Wood, author

MACAULAY, THOMAS B.

1800-1859, British historian, essayist, poet, and statesman.

He has no vision in him. He will neither see nor do any great thing, but be a poor Holland House unbeliever, with spectacles instead of eyes, to the end of him.

—Thomas Carlyle, Scottish historian,
philosopher, and essayist

He was a most disagreeable companion to my fancy . . . His conversation was a procession of one.

—Florence Nightingale, founder
of modern nursing

On Macaulay's tendencies to monopolize a conversation: You know, when I am gone you will be sorry you never heard me speak.

—Sydney Smith, English
clergyman and essayist

Macaulay is like a book in breeches . . . he has occasional flashes of silence that make his conversation perfectly delightful.

—Sydney Smith

I wish that I was as cocksure of anything as Tom Macaulay is of everything.

—William Lamb, British statesman

MacPHERSON, JAMES
1738-1796, Scottish poet

When MacPherson challenged Samuel Johnson to a duel over charges that he had "forged" his *Ossian*, he received in part this reply:

. . . I hope I shall never be deterred from detecting what I think to be a cheat, by the menaces of a ruffian.

What would you have me retract? I thought your book an imposture; I think it an imposture still . . .

Your abilities . . . are not so formidable; and what I hear of your morals, inclines me to pay regard not to what you shall say, but to what you shall prove. . . .

—Samuel Johnson, British writer, critic, and lexicographer

MAETERLINCK, MAURICE
1862-1949, Belgian dramatist, poet, and essayist

There is less in this [play] than meets the eye.

—Tallulah Bankhead, actress

MAILER, NORMAN

1923- , American writer

This gut Mailer is a hostile, narcissistic pest. Lose him.
> —Reader of *Village Voice*, complaining
> about Mailer, one of its founders

I've made an ass of myself so many times I often wonder if I am one.
> —On himself

MANSFIELD, KATHERINE

1890-1923, New Zealand author

I loathe you. . . . You revolt me stewing in your consumption . . . The Italians were quite right to have nothing to do with you.
> —D.H. Lawrence, British
> novelist and poet

MENCKEN, HENRY LOUIS

1880-1956, American editor, author, and critic

Mr. Mencken talks about truth as if she were his mistress, but he handles her like an iceman.
> —Stuart P. Sherman, American
> critic and editor

With a pig's eyes that never look up, with a pig's snout that loves muck, with a pig's brain that knows only the sty, and a pig's squeal that cries only when he is hurt, he sometimes opens his pig's mouth, tusked and ugly, and lets out the voice of God, railing at the whitewash that covers the manure about his habitat.

—William Allen White, author

MEREDITH, GEORGE

1828-1909, novelist, poet

Meredith is, to me, chiefly a stink. I should never write on him as I detest him too much ever to trust myself as critic of him.

—Ezra Pound, poet

MILLAY, EDNA ST. VINCENT

1892-1950, author

. . . the career of Edna Millay presented the still sadder spectacle of a poet who withered on the stalk before attaining fruition.

—George F. Whicher, literary biographer

MILLER, ARTHUR

1915-   , American dramatist

(Regarding his play *After the Fall*, allegedly based on his marriage to Marilyn Monroe:)
. . . a three-and-a half-hour breach of taste . . . wanton invasion of privacy . . . shameless piece of tabloid gossip, an act of exhibitionism which makes us all voyeurs . . . wretched . . . shapeless, tedious . . .

—Robert Brustein, drama critic

MILTON, JOHN
1608-1674, British poet

If its length be not considered a merit, it hath no other.

—Edmund Waller, poet

Malt does more than Milton can,
To justify God's ways to man.

—A.E. Housman, author

Read not Milton, for he is dry.

—C.S. Calverly, poet

Having never had any mental vision, he has now lost his bodily sight; a silly coxcomb, fancifying himself a beauty; an unclean beast, with nothing more human about him than his guttering eyelids; the fittest doom for him would be to hang him on the highest gallow, and set his head on the Tower of London.

—Claudius Salmasius, French
humanist and philologist

MOORE, GEORGE AUGUSTUS
1852-1933, author

He leads his readers to the latrine and locks them in.

—Oscar Wilde, British poet,
novelist, and dramatist

"Do you know George Moore?" I asked him [Oscar Wilde] one day when he had been rolling the British Zola's novels round the ring. "Know him? I know him so well that I haven't spoken to him in ten years."

—Vincent O'Sullivan, author

Susan Mitchell sensed something lacking. Women are like that. She wrote, "Some men kiss and do not tell, some kiss and tell; but George Moore told and did not kiss."

—Oliver St. John Gogarty, author

We should really be much more interested in Mr. Moore if he were not quite so interested in himself.

—G.K. Chesterton, author

MORRIS, WILLIAM

1834-1896, British poet

Of course, we all know that Morris was a wonderful all-round man, but the act of walking round him has always tired me.

—Max Beerbohm, author and caricaturist

PAINE, THOMAS

1737-1809, revolutionary, author

What a poor ignorant, malicious, short-sight, caprulous mass, is Tom Paine's *Common Sense.*

—John Adams, U.S. president

[That] mere adventurer *from England,* without fortune, without family or connections, ignorant even of grammar.

—Gouverneur Morris, American
statesman and lawyer

PARKER, DOROTHY ROTHSCHILD

1893-1967, writer, essayist

Petite, pretty, and deadly as an asp . . .

—Howard Teichmann, author

PEARSON, DREW

1897-1969, journalist and commentator

His success and power rested in large measure in the practiced impugning of others.

—Jack Anderson, newspaper columnist

There is one columnist in Washington who wouldn't have room on his breast if he got a ribbon for every time he's called a liar. In Missouri we have a four-letter word for those who knowingly make false statements.

—Harry S Truman,
U.S. president

No S.O.B. like Pearson is going to prevail on me to discharge anyone by some smart-aleck statement over the air.

—Harry S Truman

. . . a miscalled newscaster specializing in falsehoods and smearing people with personal and political motivation.

—Westbrook Pegler, journalist

He will go down in history as Pearson-the-sponge, because he gathers slime, mud and slander from all parts of the earth and lets the mud ooze out through his radio broadcasts and through his daily contributions to a few newspapers which have not found him out yet.

—Theodor Bilbo, U.S. senator

Pearson is an infamous liar, a revolting liar, a pusillanimous liar, a lying ass, a natural born liar, a liar by profession, a liar of living, a liar in the daytime, a liar in the nighttime, a dishonest, ignorant, corrupt and groveling crook.

—Kenneth McKellar, U.S. senator

Everyone makes mistakes ... but this S.O.B. makes a racket, a business, a mint of money writing fiction in the guise of news reporting.

—Walter Winchell, journalist
and commentator

He is not a sunnavabitch. He is only a filthy brain child, conceived in ruthlessness and dedicated to the proposition that Judas Iscariot was a piker.

—William Jenner, U.S. senator

Pearson is America's No. 1 keyhole peeper, muckraker, propaganda peddling prostitute of the nation's press and radio.

—William Jenner

POE, EDGAR ALLAN
1809-1849, poet, critic, author

... three-fifths of him genius and two-fifths sheer fudge ...

—James Russell Lowell, American poet,
essayist, editor, and diplomat

... an unmanly sort of man whose love-life seems to have been largely confined to crying in laps and playing house.

—W.H. Auden, poet

POPE, ALEXANDER
1688-1744, poet

His more ambitious works may be defined as careless thinking carefully verified.

—James Russell Lowell, American poet,
essayist, editor, and diplomat

He hardly drank tea without a stratagem.

—Samuel Johnson, British writer,
critic, and lexicographer

The verses, when they were written, resembled nothing so much as spoonfuls of boiling oil, ladled out by a fiendish monkey at an upstairs window upon such of the passers-by whom the wretch had a grudge against.

—Lytton Strachey, writer
and biographer

There are two ways of disliking poetry, one way is to dislike it, the other is to read Pope.

—Oscar Wilde, British poet,
novelist, and dramatist

When I hear anyone say, with definite emphasis, that Pope was a poet, I suspect him of calling in ambiguity of language to promote confusion of thought.

—A.E. Houseman, British poet
and classical scholar

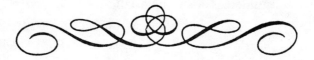

POUND, EZRA WESTON LOOMIS
1885-1972, poet

Mr. Pound is humane, but not human.

—e.e. cummings, poet

PRIOR, MATTHEW
1664-1721, poet

His Muse is, in fact a giddy wanton flirt, who spends her time in playing at snap-dragon and blind-man's buff, who tells what she should not, and knows more than she tells.

—William Hazlitt, British
essayist and critic

PULITZER, JOSEPH
1847-1911, journalist

The only consideration which guides this fellow in the control of his precious paper is to keep out of the reach of criminal prosecution.

—Leander Richardson

He was the damnedest best man in the world to have in a newspaper office for one hour in the morning. For the remainder of the day he was a damned nuisance.

—John A. Cockerill, journalist
and writer

Poor, misguided, selfish vulgarian . . .

—James Gordon Bennett, American
newspaper proprietor

REYNOLDS, QUENTIN

1902-1965, journalist and author

Quentin Reynolds has a mangy hide which was peeled and nailed to the barn door with the yellow streak glaring for the world to see.

—Westbrook Pegler, columnist

Reynolds is a celebrity who has fallen in love with himself.

—Westbrook Pegler

Reynolds is a fourflusher and a sorry mediocrity.

—Westbrook Pegler

RILEY, JAMES WHITCOMB

1849-1916, poet

. . . the unctuous, over-cheerful, word-mouthing. flabby-faced citizen who condescendingly tells Providence, in flowery and well-rounded periods, where to get off.

—Hewitt Howland, editor

ROSENTHAL, A.M.

1922-   , editor, *New York Times*

He was not . . . a passive person. He involved himself in everything. There was a Yiddish word for it: *kochleffl*, the ladle. That was Rodenthal—the *kochleffl* stirring up the poet.

—Harrison Salisbury, journalist

ROWE, NICHOLAS
1674-1718, poet, laureate, dramatist

A Gentleman, who lov'd to lie in Bed all Day for his Ease, and to sit up all Night for his Pleasure.

—John Dennis

ROSSETTI, DANTE GABRIEL
1828-1882, poet, painter

> Rossetti, dear Rossetti
> I love your work
> but you were really
> a bit of a jerk.

—George MacBeth, author

I should say that Rossetti was a man without any principles at all, who earnestly desired to find some means of salvation along the lines of least resistance.

—Ford Madox Ford, British author

RUSKIN, JOHN
1819-1900, British writer and art critic

Let not Mr. Ruskin flatter himself that more education makes the difference between himself and the policeman when both stand gazing in the Gallery.

There they might remain till the end of time; the one decently silent, the other saying, in good English, many high-sounding empty things, like the crackling of thorns under a poet—undismayed by the presence of the Masters with whose names he is sacrilegiously familar; whose intentions he interprets, whose vices he discovers with the facility of the incapable, and whose virtues he descants upon with a verbosity and flow of language that would, could he hear it, give Titian the same shock of surprise that was Balaam's, when the first great critic proferred his opinion.

—James McNeill Whistler, American
painter and etcher in England

Ruskin is one of the most turbid and fallacious minds . . . of the century. To the service of the most wildly eccentric thoughts he brings the acerbity of a bigot . . . his mental temperament is that of the first Spanish Grand Inquisitor. He is a Torquemada of aesthetics . . . He would burn alive the critic who disagrees with him.

—Max Simon Nordau, culture
critic and dramatist

SAND, GEORGE (MME DUDEVANT)

1804-1876, French novelist

In the world there are few sadder, sicklier phenomena for me than George Sand and the response she meets with . . . A new Phallus worship, with Sue, Balzac and Co., for prophets and Madame Sand for a virgin.

—Thomas Carlyle, Scottish historian,
philosopher, and essayist

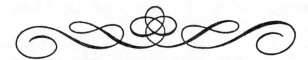

SANDBURG, CARL
1878-1967, poet

... there are moments when one is tempted to feel that the cruelest thing that happened to Lincoln since he was shot by Booth has been to fall into the hands of Carl Sandburg.

—Edmund Wilson, American
critic and author

He is submerged in adolescence ... Give Sandburg a mind, and you perhaps destroy him.

—Sherwood Anderson, American
novelist and short-story writer

SEWARD, ANNA, 'THE SWAN OF LITCHFIELD'
1747-1809, author

I did not regard Seward as exactly insincere; we generally knew at what hole she would go in, but we never felt quite sure as to where she would come out.

—Anonymous

SHAKESPEARE, WILLIAM
1564-1616, British poet and dramatist

Shakespeare boasted that as a country school master he had never blotted out a line. I wish he'd blotted out a thousand.

—Samuel Johnson, British writer,
critic, and lexicographer

Never did any author precipitate himself from such heights of thought to so low expressions, as he often does. He is the very *Janus* of poets; he wears, almost everywhere two faces: and you have scarce begun to admire the one, e'er you despise the other.

—John Dryden, British poet,
critic, and dramatist

A sycophant, a flatterer, a breaker of marriage vows, a whining and inconstant person.

—Ebenezer Forsyth, author

I cannot read him, he is such a bombast fellow.

—George II, king of England
(attributed)

. . . a vulgar, illiterate . . . deerpoacher, and Lord Leicester's stableboy.

—Delia Bacon, author

With the single exception of Homer, there is no eminent writer, not even Sir Walter Scott, whom I can despise so entirely as I despise Shakespeare when I measure my mind against his. The intensity of my impatience with him occasionally reaches such pitch, that it would positively be a relief to me to dig him up and throw stones at him, knowing as I do, how incapable he and his worshippers are of understanding any less obvious form of indignity.

—G.B. Shaw, Irish dramatist and critic

. . . we saw *Midsummer Night's Dream*, which I had never seen before, nor shall ever see again, for it is the most insipid, ridiculous play that I ever saw in my life.

—Samuel Pepys, British diarist
and government official

The undisputed fame enjoyed by Shakespeare as a writer
. . . is, like every other lie, a great evil.

—Count Leo Tolstoy, author

SHAW, GEORGE BERNARD

1856-1950, Irish dramatist and critic

Bernard Shaw hasn't an enemy in the world— and none
of his friends like him.

—Oscar Wilde, British poet,
novelist, and dramatist

—Oh dear me—it's too late to do anything but *accept* you
and *love* you—but when you were quite a little boy somebody ought to have said "hush" just once.

—Mrs. Patrick Campbell, British actress

[Shaw presents commonplace ideas] "so scandalously that
the pious get all the thrills out of the business that would ac-
company a view of the rector in liquor in the pulpit."

—H.L. Mencken, American
writer, editor, and critic

His brain is a half-inch layer of champagne poured over a
bucket of Methodist near-beer.

—Benjamin de Casseres, author

Shaw is a Puritan who missed the *Mayflower* by five
minutes.

—Benjamin de Casseres

Written exchange between the Irish playwright and the future prime minister. Shaw enclosed two tickets:
Bring a friend if you have one.
Churchill returned the tickets, requesting them for the second performance:
If there is one.

—Winston Churchill, British
prime minister

Intellectually he is beneath contempt. Artistically he appeals only to pseudo-philosophers . . . Are we not all a little tired of this blatant self-puffery?

—Alfred Noyes, poet

The way Bernard Shaw believes in himself is very refreshing in these atheistic days when so many people believe in no god at all.

—Israel Zangwill, novelist and critic

An Irish smut-dealer.

—Anthony Comstock, U.S. social reformer

An idiot child screaming in a hospital.

—H.G. Wells, British novelist

A desiccated bourgeois . . a fossilized chauvinist, a self-satisfied Englishman.

—*Pravda*

A freakish homunculus germinated outside lawful procreation.

—Henry Arthur Jones, British dramatist

George Bernard Shaw, most poisonous of all the poisonous haters of England; despiser, distorter and denier of the plain truths whereby men live; topsyturvy perverter of all human relationships; menace to ordered social thought and ordered social life; irresponsible braggart, blaring self-trumpeter; idol of opaque intellectuals and thwarted females; calculus of contrariwise; flippertygibbet pope of chaos; portent and epitome of this generation's moral and spiritual disorder.

—Henry Arthur Jones

SHELLEY, PERCY BYSSHE

1792-1822, poet

A beautiful and ineffectual angel, beating in the void his luminous wings in vain.

—Matthew Arnold, British poet,
critic, and essayist

A lewd vegetarian.

—Charles Kingsley, clergyman
and author

Shelley is a poor creature, who has said or done nothing worth a serious man being at the trouble of remembering . . . Poor soul, he has always seemed to me an extremely weak creature; a poor, thin, spasmodic, hectic, shrill and pallid being . . . The very voice of him, shrill, shrieky, to my ear has too much of the ghost!

—Thomas Carlyle, Scottish historian,
philosopher, and essayist

SHERIDAN, RICHARD B.

1751-1816, Irish dramatist and politician

Sherry is dull, naturally dull; but it must have taken him a great deal of pain to become what we now see him. Such an excess of stupidity, sir, is not in nature.

—Samuel Johnson, British writer,
lexicographer, and critic

SITWELL, DAME EDITH

1887-1864, authoress

Then Edith Sitwell appeared, her nose longer than an anteater's, and read some of her absurd stuff.

—Lytton Strachey, British biographer

The Sitwells belong to the history of publicity rather than of poetry.

—F.R. Leavis, author

SMART, CHRISTOPHER

1722-1771, British poet

On the comparative talents of the poets [Samuel Derrick and Christopher Smart]: Sir, there is no setting the point of precedency between a louse and a flea.

—Samuel Johnson, English writer,
critic, and lexicographer

SOCRATES

470-399 B.C., philosopher

The more I read him, the less I wonder why they poisoned him.

—T.B. Macaulay, British historian,
poet, essayist, and statesman

SOUTHEY, ROBERT

1774-1843, British poet laureate

He had sung against all battles, and again
   In their high praise and glory; he had call'd
Reviewing "the ungentle craft," and then
   Become as base a critic as ever crawled—
Fed, paid, and pamp'd by the very men
   By whom his muse and morals had been
      maul'd:
He had written much blank verse, and blanker
      prose,
   And more of both than anybody knows.

—Lord Byron, poet

SPENCER, HERBERT

1820-1903, British philosopher

The most unending ass in Christendom.

—Thomas Carlyle, Scottish historian,
philosopher, and essayist

STEIN, GERTRUDE

1874-1946, poet, expatriate author

What an old covered-wagon she is!

—F. Scott Fitzgerald,
American novelist

Reading Gertrude Stein at length is not unlike making one's way through an interminable and badly printed game book.

—Richard Bridgeman, author

Gertrude Stein is the mama of dada.

—Clifton Fadiman, critic

Miss Stein was a past master in making nothing happen very slowly.

—Clifton Fadiman

The supreme egocentric of the most perfect clique of egocentrics.

—Oscar Cargill, professor and literary critic

STOWE, HARRIET BEECHER

1812-1896, novelist

A blatant Bassarid of Boston, a rampant Maenad of Massachusetts.

—A.G. Swinburne, poet

STRACHEY, (GILES) LYTTON
1880-1932, author, historian

Incapable of creation in life or in literature, his writings were a substitute for both.

—T.R. Barnes, author

SWIFT, JONATHAN
1667-1745, Irish satirist and man of letters

The reader of the fourth part of *Gulliver's Travels* is like the hero himself in this instance. It is Yahoo language, a monster gibbering shrieks, and gnashing imprecations against mankind—tearing down all shreds of modesty, past all sense of manliness and shame; filthy in word, filthy in thought, furious raging, obscene.

—William Makepeace Thackeray,
British novelist and critic

SWINBURNE, ALGERNON CHARLES
1837-1909, British poet

All that is worst in Mr. Swinburne belongs to Baudelaire. The offensive choice of subject, the obtrusion of unnatural passion, the blasphemy, the wretched animals, are all taken intact out of the Fleurs du Mal. Pitiful! that any sane man, least of all an English poet, should think this dunghill worthy of importation!

—Robert Buchanan, poet
and novelist

I attempt to describe Mr. Swinburne; and lo! the Bacchanal screams, the sterile Dolores sweats, serpents dance, men and women wrench, wriggle, and foam in an endless alliteration of heated and meaningless words.

—Robert Buchanan

He was certainly an odd, scarcely human, figure.

—Richard Le Gallienne,
British man of letters

. . . a perfect leper, and a mere sodomite.

—Ralph Waldo Emerson, American
essayist, philosopher, and poet

I have no wish to know anyone sitting in a sewer and adding to it.

—Thomas Carlyle, Scottish historian,
philosopher, and essayist

TENNYSON, ALFRED LORD
1809-1892, British poet laureate

Tennyson is a beautiful half of a poet.

—Ralph Waldo Emerson, American essayist,
philosopher, and poet

Brahms is just like Tennyson, an extraordinary musician with the brains of a third-rate village policeman.

—G.B. Shaw, Irish playwright

THACKERAY, WILLIAM MAKEPEACE
1811-1863, British novelist

No one succeeds better than Mr. Thackeray in cutting his coat according to his cloth. Here he flattered the aristocracy; but when he crossed the Atlantic, George Washington became the idol of his worship, the "Four Georges" the objects of his bitterest attacks.
. . . There is a want of heart in all he writes, which is not to be balanced by the most brilliant sarcasm and the most perfect knowledge of the working of the human heart.

—Edmund Yates, English
editor and novelist

George Smythe said, that, as they say, novelists always draw their own characters, he wished Thackeray would draw his own—that would be a character! The Cynic Parasite!

—Benjamin Disraeli, British
prime minister

Thackeray settled like a meat-fly on whatever one had got for dinner, and made one sick of it.

—John Ruskin, British writer, art
critic, and social reformer

THOMAS, DYLAN MARLAIS
1914-1953, poet

His passion for lies was congenital.

—Caitlin Thomas, author

In America, visiting British writers are greeted at cocktail parties by faculty wives with "Can you screw as good as Dylan?"

—Anthony Burgess, author

THOREAU, HENRY DAVID

1817-1862, essayist, poet, transcendentalist

He was imperfect, unfinished, inartistic, he was worse than provincial—he was parochial.

—Henry James, American
novelist and critic

Behind a mask of self-exaltation Thoreau performed as before a mirror—and first of all for his own edification. He was a fragile Narcissus embodied in a homely New Englander.

—Leon Edel, author
and biographer

TOLSTOY, LEO NIKOLAYEVICH

1828-1910, novelist and social theorist

The truth is if Tolstoy would live across the street, I wouldn't go to see him. I would rather read what he writes.

—Isaac Bashevis Singer, author

TONSON, JACOB
1656?-1736, British publisher

> With leering Looks, Bull-fac'd, and freckl'd fair,
> With two legs, and Judas-color'd Hair,
> And frowzy Pores that taint the ambient Air.

> —John Dryden, British
> poet laureate

TROLLOPE, ANTHONY
1815-1882, novelist

He has a gross and repulsive face and manner, but appears *bon enfant* when you talk with him. But he is the dullest Briton of them all.

> —Henry James, American
> novelist and critic

TWAIN, MARK
(SAMUEL LANGHORNE CLEMENS)
1835-1910, writer and humorist

. . . a hack writer who would not have been considered fourth rate in Europe, who tricked out a few of the old proven "sure fire" literary skeletons with sufficient local color to intrigue the superficial and the lazy.

> —William Faulkner, author

His wife not only edited his works but edited him.

> —Van Wyck Brooks, author

VOLTAIRE, FRANÇOIS MARIE AROUET DE

1694-1778, French dramatist, poet, philosopher

He is like the false Amphytrion; although a stranger, it is always he who has the air of being master of the house.

—Guillaume Dubuc, French pastor

Here lies the child spoiled by the world which he spoiled.

—Baroness de Montolieu
(epitaph of Voltaire)

WALPOLE, HORACE, FOURTH EARL OF ORFORD

1717-1797, author

The conformation of his mind was such that whatever was little seemed to him great, and whatever was great seemed to him little.

—T.B. Macaulay, British historian,
poet, essayist, and statesman

How *cooooold* he be ainy goood? He knows naaaathing about saix!

—Robertson Nicoll, British
literary scholar

WAUGH, EVELYN

1903-1966, author

So Evelyn Waugh is in his coffin. Died of snobbery.

—Cecil Beaton, in *Selected
Portraits with Friends*

WEBSTER, NOAH

1758-1843, lexicographer

It is a melancholy proof of the amount of mischief one man of learning can do to society, that Webster's system of orthography is adopted and propagated.

—William Cullen Bryant, American
poet and journalist

In conversation he is even duller than in writing, if that is possible.

—Juliana Smith

WELLES, HERBERT GEORGE

1866-1946, author

The tragedy of H.G.'s life—his aptitude for "fine thinking" and even "good feeling" and yet his total incapacity for decent conduct.

—Beatrice Webb, British
social economist

WHITMAN, WALT

1819-1892, poet

Under the dirty clumsy paws of a harper whose plectrum is a muckrake, any tune will become a chaos of dischords . . . Mr. Whitman's Eve is a drunken apple-woman, indecently sprawling in the slush and garbage of the gutter amid the rotten refuse of her overturned fruit-stall: but Mr. Whitman's Venus is a Hottentot wench under the influence of cantharides and adulterated rum.

—Algernon Charles Swinburne,
English poet and critic

This awful Whitman. This post-mortem poet. This poet with the private soul leaking out of him all the time. All his privacy leaking out in a sort of dribble, oozing into the universe.

—D.H. Lawrence, novelist

WILDE, OSCAR FINGAL O'FLAHERTIE WILLS
1854-1900, author, dramatist, wit

That sovereign of insufferables.

—Ambrose Bierce, American writer

From the beginning Wilde performed his life and continued to do so even after fate had taken the plot out of his hands.

—W.H. Auden, British poet
in the U.S.

Oscar Wilde's talent seems to me essentially rootless, something growing in a glass in a little water.

—George Moore, Irish novelist,
dramatist, and critic

He was, on his plane, as insufferable as a Methodist is on his.

—H.L. Mencken, American writer,
editor, and critic

WILMOT, JOHN, EARL OF ROCHESTER
1647-1680, poet, libertine

Lord Rochester's poems have much more obscenity than wit, more wit than poetry, more poetry than politeness.

—Horace Walpole, British writer

WINCHELL, WALTER
1897-1972, journalist

Poor Walter. He's afraid he'll wake up some day and discover he's not Walter Winchell.

—Dorothy Parker, American short-
story and verse writer

This is a dangerously ill-informed man who, in his tremendous egotism, who, with this great power, unaccompanied by greatness or nobility of thinking, is uttering sage opinions on what we should do . . . .

—Ed Sullivan, television personality

"A Gent's Room journalist."

—Westbrook Pegler, journalist

I don't see why Walter Winchell is allowed to live.

—Ethel Barrymore, actress

WOOLLCOTT, ALEXANDER HUMPHREYS
1887-1943, author, critic

He looked like something that had gotten loose from Macy's Thanksgiving Day Parade.

—Harpo Marx, comedian

Woollcott's criticism may be "simply pathological in origin" or owing to Pa's too high blood pressure perhaps, an unfortunate chronic costiveness. Woolcott's approach is "lump in the throat reviewing."

—George Jean Nathan,
novelist and critic

WOOLF, (ADELINE) VIRGINIA
1882-1941, novelist

Virginia Woolf seemed to have the worst defect of the Mandarin style, the ability to spin cocoons of language out of nothing.

—Cyril Connolly, author

Virginia Woolf, I enjoyed talking to her, but thought *nothing* of her writing. I considered her "a beautiful little knitter."

—Edith Sitwell, British
poet and critic

WORDSWORTH, WILLIAM
1770-1850, British poet

One finds also a kind of *sincerity* in his speech. But for prolixity, thinness, endless dilution, it excels all the other speeches I had heard from mortals. A genuine man, which is much, but also essentially a small genuine man ... The languid way in which he gives you a handful of numb unresponsive fingers is very significant.

—Thomas Carlyle, Scottish historian,
philosopher, and essayist

In his youth, Wordsworth sympathized with the French Revolution, went to France, wrote good poetry, and had a natural daughter. At this period, he was called a "bad" man.

Then he became "good," abandoned his daughter, adopted correct principles, and wrote bad poetry.

—Bertrand Russell, philosopher

Dank, liber verses, stuft with lakeside sedges,
And propt with rotten stakes from rotten hedges.
—Walter Savage Landor,
British author

Two voices are there: one is of the deep;
It learns the storm-cloud's thunderous melody . . .
And one is of an old half-witted sheep
Which bleats articulate monotony . . .
And, Wordsworth, both are thine.
—James Kenneth Stephen, poet

What a beastly and pitiful wretch that Wordsworth . . . I can compare him with no one but Simonides, that flatterer of the Sycillian tyrants.
—Percy Bysshe Shelley, poet

Mr. Wordsworth, a stupid man, with a decided gift for portraying nature in vignettes, never yet ruined anyone's morals, unless, perhaps, he has driven some susceptible persons to crime in a very fury of boredom.
—Ezra Pound, poet

Chapter Five

• • • •

FINE ARTISTS
AND ENTERTAINERS

On the whole, the slings and arrows of outrageous insults have been flung less often at fine artists than at writers. A painting or piece of sculpture has a less immediate impact than the written word. Similarly, a musical composition is not as well suited to a slur or affront as an article, an essay, a newspaper column, a book. In fact, in order to spew forth their own venom fine artists have usually had to resort to the article, the essay, the column.

Artists have their feuds, peeves, likes and dislikes, and try no harder than others to suppress them. When insults to artists have come from outside sources, such as critics, they have dealt more often than not with the introduction of "new" or "modern" forms of art. Abstract art has drawn particular fire. Picasso, Matisse, Klee, and others have been the recipients of many remarks questioning especially their sanity.

Entertainers have been highly visible and equally highly

paid, making them the object of many insults. A goodly share is rooted in envy of their good looks, sex appeal, fame, wealth. But envy has come from within as well as without, for entertainers and actors also have big egos. Their reputation for self-adoration and Don Juanism has made it easy to develop appropriate barbs.

ALI, MOHAMMED (CASSIUS CLAY)
1942-   , boxing champion

. . . I say he's a loudmouth. He makes a bunch of noise. He says I'm a Tom, that I don't stand up for the black man. . . . What does he know about hard times? He had it easy in boxing. A white man in his corner, those rich plantation owners to back him and a white lawyer to keep him out of jail and he's going to Uncle Tom me. I have a black man in my corner, my manager, and both black and white people backing me.

—Joe Frazier, boxing champion

ALLEN, FRED (JOHN FLORENCE SULLIVAN)
1894-1956, comedian

I don't have to look up my family tree, because I know that I'm the sap.

—On himself

ALMA-TADEMA, SIR LAWRENCE
1836-1912, British painter

The general effect was exactly like a microscopic view of a small detachment of black beetles, in search of a dead rat.

—John Ruskin, British writer, art critic, and social reformer

ARNE, THOMAS AUGUSTINE
1710-1778, composer

I have read your play and rode your horse, and do not approve of either. They both want particular spirit which alone can give pleasure to the reader and the rider. When the one wants wits, and the other the spur, they both job on very heavily. I must keep the horse, but I have returned you the play. I pretend to some little knowledge of the last; but as I am no jockey, they cannot say that the knowing one is taken in.

—David Garrick, British actor and theater manager

BANKHEAD, TALLULAH BROCKMAN
1903-1968, Actress

Tallulah Bankhead barged down the Nile last night as Cleopatra—and sank.

—John Mason Brown, critic

A day away from Tallulah Bankhead is like a month in the country.

—Anonymous

I'm as pure as driven slush.

—On herself

Dorothy Parker gave a party one night at the Algonquin, and guest Tallulah Bankhead, slightly inebriated, carried on in a wild indecorous manner. After Miss Bankhead had been escorted out, Mrs. Parker called in from an adjoining room, "Has Whistler's Mother left yet?"

The next day at lunch Tallulah took out a pocket mirror, examined herself painfully, and said, with a glance at Mrs. Parker, "The less I behave like Whistler's Mother the night before, the more I look like her the morning after."

—Robert E. Drennan, author

Watching Tallulah Bankhead on the stage is like watching somebody skating over very thin ice—and the English want to be there when she falls through.

—Mrs. Patrick Campbell,
English actress

BARA, THEDA
1890-1955, actress

Miss Bara made voluptuousness a common American commodity, as accessible as chewing gum.

—Lloyd Morris, author

BARKER, HARLEY GRANVILLE
1877-1946, actor and dramatist

Oh, G.B., you are a very clever and interesting youth of 30; but you are an atrocious manager. You don't know where to put your high light and where to put your smudge.

—G.B. Shaw, Irish dramatist
and critic

BARNUM, PHINEAS TAYLOR
1810-1891, impresario

He will ultimately take his stand in the social rank ... among the swindlers, blacklegs, pickpockets, and thimble-riggers of his day.

—Anonymous

BEARDSLEY, AUBREY VINCENT
1872-1898, artist, author

... a face like a silver hatchet, with grass-green hair.

—Oscar Wilde, British poet,
novelist, and dramatist

BEECHAM, SIR THOMAS
1879-1961, conductor

... I never heard him refer to religion. To women he referred once, saying that none of them was worth the loss of a night's sleep.

—Neville Cardus, author

I have always been noted for my instability. I am a very, very low brow.

—On himself

BEETHOVEN, LUDWIG VAN
1770-1827, composer

Beethoven always sounds to me like the upsetting of a bag of nails, with here and there an also dropped hammer.

—John Ruskin, British writer, art critic, and social reformer

BENCHLEY, ROBERT CHARLES
1889-1945, humorist, critic, actor

I do most of my work sitting down; that's where I shine.

—On himself

When he died, one of them said, "They're going to have to stay up late in heaven now."

—James Thurber, author

Robert Benchley has a style that is weak and lies down frequently to rest.

—Max Eastman, author

Merely as an observer of natural phenomena, I am fascinated by my own personal appearance. This does not mean that I am pleased with it, mind you, or that I can even tolerate it. I simply have a morbid interest in it.

—On himself

Drawing on my fine command of language I said nothing.

—On himself

BENNY, JACK (BENJAMIN KUBELSKY)
1894-1974, comedian

I don't want to say that Jack Benny is cheap, but he's got short arms and carries his money low in his pockets.

—Fred Allen, comedian

When Jack Benny plays the violin, it sounds as if the strings are still back in the cat.

—Fred Allen

Is Mr. Benny tight? Well, a little snug, perhaps . . . If he can't take it with him, he ain't gonna go.

—Eddie "Rochester" Anderson,
comedian

You know, Jack's show did a lot for the image of black people in America. You ready? Before Jack came along, everybody thought blacks were only fit to be shoeshine boys and railroad porters. The Jack Benny program proved to Americans that they could also be chauffeurs, dishwashers, houseboys!

—Demond Wilson, actor
and comedian

BERGMAN, INGRID
1915-   , actress

My friend feels that this is not acting—this is me.

—On her role as a career
mother in *Autumn Sonata*

BERLE, MILTON

1908-   , comedian

Walter Winchell, angry at comedian Milton Berle who had a reputation for "stealing" the jokes of fellow-comedians, referred to Berle as "The Thief of Bad Gags."

—Walter Winchell, news commentator

BERNHARDT, SARAH

1844-1923, French actress

An empty cab drove up and Sarah Bernhardt got out.

—Arthur Bugs Baer

BETTY, WILLIAM HENRY WEST

1791-1874, actor

Betty is performing here, I fear, very ill; his figure is that of a hippopotamus, his face like the bull and mouth on the panels of a heavy coach, his arms are fins fattened out of shape, his voice the gargling of an alderman with the quinsy, and his acting altogether ought to be natural, for it certainly is like nothing that Art has ever yet exhibited on the stage.

—Lord Byron, poet

BEWICK, THOMAS

1753-1828, wood engraver, author, naturalist

He could draw a pig, but not an Aphrodite.

—John Ruskin, British writer, art critic, and social reformer

BOOTH, JOHN WILKES

1838-1865, actor, assassin of Lincoln

He was mad with his own ego, possessed of a theatrical vanity that gnawed incessantly for fame.

—Jay Robert Nash, author

BULL, JOHN

1563-1628, composer

Of all the bulls that lie, this hath the greatest asses' ears.

—Elizabeth I, attributed

BYRD, WILLIAM

1543-1623, composer

Byrd's misfortune is that when he is not first-rate he is so rarely second-rate . . .

—Gustav Holst, British composer

CAMPBELL, MRS. PATRICK (BEATRICE STELLA)

1865-1940, actress

If only you could write a true book, entitled *Why, though I was a wonderful actress, no manager or author would ever engage me twice if he could possibly help it,* it would be a bestseller. But you couldn't. Besides, you don't know. I do.

—G.B. Shaw, Irish dramatist
and critic

CARSON, JOHNNY
1925-   , television personality

It has always been my personal conviction that Carson is the most overrated amateur since Evelyn and her magic violin.

—Rex Reed, U.S. film critic

CÉZANNE, PAUL
1839-1906, French post-Impressionist painter

M. Cézanne must be some kind of a lunatic, afflicted with delirium tremens while he is painting. In fact, it is one of those weird shapes, thrown off by hashish, borrowed from a swarm of ridiculous dreams.

—Anonymous French critic

COSELL, HOWARD
1920-   , sports announcer

Don Klosterman once called over to Roone Arledge, then head of ABC sports: "Hey, Roone, . . . come over and help me listen to Howard."

—Don Kosterman, television
sports personality

In the next issue of *Cosmopolitan*, Howard Cosell will be the centerfold with his vital organ covered—his mouth.

—Burt Reynolds, actor

DAVIS, SAMMY, JR.

1925- , singer, actor

I hope I'll recognize you in the synagogue.

> —Samuel Goldwyn, sarcastically
> to Sammy, a recent convert to
> Judaism, after he requested to
> be off to observe Yom Kippur

DAVISON, JO

1883-1952, sculptor

I had brought some photos of my sculpture. Ghandi looked at them intently and said: "I see you make heroes out of mud." And I retorted: "And sometimes vice-versa."

> —On himself

ELGAR, SIR EDWARD WILLIAM

1857-1934, composer

It is all so original, so individual and subjective that it will take the British public 10 years to let it soak into its pachydermal mind . . .

> —A.J. Jaeger

Edward Elgar, the figurehead of music in England, is a composer whose rank it is neither prudent nor indeed possible to determine. Either it is one so high that only time and posterity can confer it, or else he is one of the Seven Humbugs of Christendom.

> —G.B. Shaw, Irish dramatist
> and critic

ELLISTON ROBERT WILLIAM
1774-1831, actor

A wretched Tragedian . . . his attempts at dignity are ludicrous. He is a fine bustling comedian but he bustles in tragedy also.

—Henry Crabb Robinson, British diarist and journalist

His feelings follow each other like the buckets on a water-wheel, full one instant and empty the next.

—Leigh Hunt, British poet, critic, and journalist

EPSTEIN, SIR JACOB
1880-1959, sculptor

From life's grim nightmare he is now released
Who saw in every face the lurking beast.
"A loss to Art," say friends both proud and loyal,
"A loss," say others, "to the Café Royal."

—Anonymous

. . . I've seen the Epstein. My dear fellow! . . . I confess it makes me physically a little sick. The wretched woman has two sets of breasts and hip joints like a merry thought! No, really!

—John Galsworthy, novelist and playwright

Epstein is a great sculptor. I·wish he would wash, but I believe Michel Angelso *never* did, so I suppose it is part of the tradition.

—Ezra Pound, poet

ERLANGER, A.L.

1860-1930, theater producer

A.L. Erlanger I believe to be a brutal bully. . . His dominance of the American stage is a disgrace. He is an incubus upon that institution.

—William Winter, theater critic

FAIRBANKS, DOUGLAS

1883-1939, actor

He died at fifty-six in 1939, his tanned body apparently untouched by age, but actually so muscle-bound that the blood could barely circulate. He had not so much died, some friends thought, as run down.

—John Baxter, author

Doug was so energetic, so frenetic, so able to run extremely fast in the wrong direction that he was the perfect figure to embody a human trait gone frenziedly wrong.

—Gerald Mast, author

Douglas had always faced a situation the only way he knew how, by running away from it.

—Mary Pickford, actress

Thomas Edison devoted his life to machines intended to make thinking unnecessary for the masses. Fairbanks is devoting his to pictures calculated to keep their minds off the fact that they do not think.

—Terry Ramsaye, film
writer and historian

FLYNN, ERROL LESLIE

1909-1959, actor

He had a mediocre talent, but to all the Walter Mittys of the world he was all the heroes in one magnificent, sexy, animal package.

—Jack L. Warner, movie producer

FOOTE, SAMUEL

1720-1777, actor, dramatist

> Now in the centre, now in van or rear,
> The Proteus shifts, bawd, parson, auctioneer,
> His stokes of humour, and his bursts of sport
> Are all contain'd in this one word, *distort*.

—Charles Churchill, British
poet and satirist

Foote is quite impartial, for he tells lies of everybody.

—Samuel Johnson, British writer,
critic, and lexicographer

There is a witty satirical story of Foote. He had a small bust of Garrick placed upon his bureau. "You may be surprised (said he), that I allow him to be so near my gold;—but you will observe, he has no hands."

—Samuel Johnson

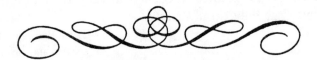

FORD, JOHN (SEAN O'FEENEY)

1895-1973, motion picture director

John is half-tyrant, half-revolutionary; half saint, half-satan; half-possible, half-impossible; half-genius, half-Irish —but *all* director and *all* American.

—Frank Capra, film director

FROST, DAVID

1939-   , television personality

I always felt Frost was totally absorbed with himself and had a synthetic personality with a fixed smile carefully adapted to the slick phoniness of ad-agency types, show-business types and broadcast-executive types.

—Howard Cosell, sports announcer

GAINSBOROUGH, THOMAS

1727-1788, painter

His subjects are softened and sentimentalized too much; it is not simple unaffected nature that we see, but nature sitting for her picture.

—William Hazlitt, British
essayist and critic

GARLAND, JUDY

1922-1969, actress

I am Mr. Mayer's little hunchback.

—On herself, referring to
L.B. Mayer of MGM

GERSHWIN, GEORGE
1898-1937, American composer

George Gershwin played good tennis almost by ear.

—Oscar Levant, American pianist,
actor, and wit

Tell me, George, if you had it to do all over again, would you fall in love with yourself again?

—Oscar Levant

GRABLE, (ELIZABETH RUTH) BETTY
1916-1973, actress

Miss Grable's beauty—if that is the word for it—was of the common sort. Nor did she offer much in the way of character maturity. She was, at best, a sort of great American floozie, and her appeal to lonely GIs was surely that of every hash-house waitress with whom they ever flirted.

—Richard Schickel, film critic

GREENOUGH, HORATIO
1805-1852, sculptor

[Greenough's] tongue was far cunninger in talk than his chisel [was] to carve.

—Ralph Waldo Emerson, American
essayist, philosopher, and poet

HARLOW, JEAN (HARLEAN CARPENTER)
1911-1937, actress

There is no sign that her acting would ever have progressed beyond the scope of the restless shoulders and the protuberant breasts; her technique was the gangster's technique—she toted a breast like a man totes a gun.

—Graham Greene, author

HAYES, WOODY
1913-   , Ohio State football coach

In addition to working my ass off the way no assistant coach ever dreamed of working, they said I'd have the privilege of experiencing Woody's minitons, megatons, and hundred megatons. His staff measures his rages that way.

—Ed Ferkany, former Ohio State
University line coach

He favors the running game because it favors those who can administer and absorb pain, two abilities that mark life's winners. "If it comes easy," Hayes says, "it isn't worth a damn." He thinks the forward pass is a modernist heresy, worse than gun control and almost as bad as deficit spending.

—George Will, political columnist

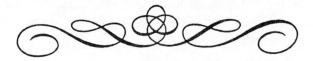

HEPBURN, KATHERINE

1909-   , actress

Katharine Hepburn ran the whole gamut of emotions from A to B.

—Dorothy Parker, journalist
and critic

IRVING, SIR HENRY

1838-1905, actor

Somebody asked Gilbert if he had been to see Irving in *Faust*. "I go to the pantomime," said Gilbert, "only at Christmas."

—Leslie Ayre, expert on
Gilbert and Sullivan

He does not merely cut plays, he disembowels them.

—George Bernard Shaw, Irish
dramatist and critic

Of the theatre at large he knew almost nothing; for he never left his own stage.

—George Bernard Shaw

JACOBS, MIKE

1880-1953, boxing promoter

About Jacobs it was once written: "Jacobs himself was a curmudgeonish product of the rough-and-tumble life of Broadway, along which he had achieved a reputation as the most resourceful speculator in the theatrical district. He was hard-crusted and crafty and totally without formal education. When he was in need of a favor, he was charming and warm and obliging, almost to the point of sycophancy; otherwise he was a ruthless predator who had struggled up from poverty on New York's lower West Side. . . ."

—Barney Nagler, author

JOLSON, AL (ASA YOELSON)
1888-1950, singer, actor

It was easy enough to make Jolson happy at home. You just had to cheer him for breakfast, applaud wildly for lunch, and give him a standing ovation for dinner.

—George Burns, comedian

KARLOFF, BORIS (WILLIAM HENRY PRATT)
1887-1969, actor

Like the late Lon Chaney, he reached stardom with the sole assistance of the make-up man.

—Graham Greene, author

KEAN, CHARLES JOHN
1811-1868, actor

His tone is somewhat dogmatic, but I prefer him in the dining room to him on the stage.

—Henry Crabb Robinson, British
diarist and journalist

KEAN, EDMUND
1787-1833, actor

He had no gaiety; he could not laugh; he had no playfulness that was not the playfulness of a panther showing her claws every moment.

—George Henry Lewes, British
critic and author

KEMBLE, JOHN PHILIP
1757-1823, actor

Frogs in a marsh, flies in a bottle, wind in a crevice, a preacher in a field, the drone of a bagpipe, all yielded to the inimitable soporific monotony of Mr. Kemble.

—George Coleman, British dramatist

KENNEDY, JACQUELINE
1929-   , wife of U.S. President John Kennedy

. . . forever locked into our National Family Soap Opera.

—Ellen Goodman, columnist

KENT, WILLIAM
1686-1748, architect

William Kent was one of those generally accomplished persons who can do everything up to a certain point, and nothing well.

—Sir Reginald Bloomfield, author

LADD, ALAN WALBRIDGE
1913-1964, actor

Hard, bitter and occasionally charming, he is after all a small boy's idea of a tough.

—Raymond Thorton Chandler,
American detective-story writer

No one ever pretended that he could act. He got to the top, therefore, by a combination of determination and luck.

—David Shipman, British
film critic

LAUGHTON, CHARLES
1899-1962, actor

We got on very well—in spite of his strange habits, such as a terrific prejudice concerning Jews and needing strange off-stage noises to get himself in the mood for acting. He was the first actor I encountered who prepared to make a laughing entrance by going around doing ha-ha! sounds for hours.

—George Cukor, film director

He was a big, brazen, show-off actor. He went overboard sometimes and, in some of the poor films he made, he got near to chewing the scenery. . .

—David Shipman, British film critic

LOMBARDI, VINCE

1913-1978, football coach

He treated all players the same—like dogs.

—a former player

LOUIS, JOE (JOSEPH LOUIS BARROW)

1914-   , American boxer

The black man will always be afraid of me . . . He is inferior.

—Max Schmeling, heavyweight champion
(remarks falsely attributed to him
by the Nazi press)

LUGOSI, BELA

1882-1956, actor

For some people, he was the embodiment of dark, mysterious forces, a harbinger of evil from the world of shadow. For others he was merely a ham actor appearing in a type of film unsuitable for children and often unfit for adults.

—Arthur Lenning, Lugosi's biographer

MICHELANGELO
(MICHELANGELO BUONARROTI)

1475-1564, Italian painter, sculptor, architect, poet

A Pietà was uncovered at S. Spirito, which a Florentine . . . sent to that church. It is sad that the original was the work of that inventor of filthiness, who cared more for art than for devotion, Michelangelo. All the modern painters and sculptors have brought matters to such a pitch that . . . I hope . . . God will one day send His saints and dash to earth idolatrous images like these.

—a Florentine citizen

MILLAIS, SIR JOHN EVERETT
1829-1896, artist

This strangely unequal painter—a painter whose imperfectly great powers always suggest to me the legend of the spiteful fairy at the christening feast. The name of Mr. Millais's spiteful fairy is vulgarity.

—Henry James, American novelist
and essayist in England

MILLS, ROBERT
1781-1855, architect, engineer

As for his syntax, it never troubles those who leave it alone.

—Douglas Bush, author

MORSE, SAMUEL FINLEY BREESE
1791-1872, artist, inventor

He makes good portraits, strong likenesses; . . . but he cannot design. There is no poetry about his paintings, and his prose consists of straight lines, which look as if they have been stretched to their utmost tension to form clothes-lines.

—Philip Hone, American
diarist and politician

MIX, (THOMAS HEZEKIAH) TOM

1880-1940, actor

They say he rides like part of the horse, but they don't say what part.

—Robert E. Sherwood,
American dramatist

NAMATH, JOSEPH

1943-   , football player

Joe has a great respect for girls. Only last week in New York, he saved a girl from being attacked. He controlled himself.

—Dean Martin, singer,
actor, and comedian

OLIVIER, SIR LAURENCE

1907-   , actor

Sometimes I think I'll not be remembered for Hamlet nor Richard III. Nor even *Wuthering Heights*. Sometimes I think a whole generation of youngsters will know me only as "that man who did the Polaroid commercials."

—On himself

PARRY, SIR CHARLES HUBERT HASTINGS

1848-1918, composer

It is a good thing Parry died when he did; otherwise he might have set the whole Bible to music.

—Frederick Delius, British composer

I cannot stand Parry's orchestra: it's dead and never more than an *organ part arranged.*

—Edward Elgar, British composer

PAXTON, SIR JOSEPH
1801-1865, architect, landscape designer

His life was simple, his ingenuity unfailing, his energy unbounded, his health robust, his taste dubious.

—R. Furneaux-Jordan, author

PRESLEY, ELVIS ARON
1935-1977, singer

Mr. Presley has no discernible singing ability. His specialty is rhythm songs which he renders in an undistinguished whine; his phrasing, if it can be called that, consists of the stereotyped variations that go with a beginner's aria in a bathtub. For the ear he is an unutterable bore. . . .

—Jack Gould, journalist and
television commentator

Mr. Presley made another television appearance last night on the Milton Berle show over Channel 4 . . . he might possibly be classified as an entertainer. Or, perhaps quite as easily as an assignment for a sociologist.

—Jack Gould

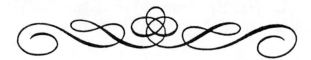

RENOIR, PIERRE-AUGUSTE

1841-1919, French painter

Just explain to Monsieur Renoir that the torso of a woman is not a mass of decomposing flesh, its green and violet spots indicating the state of complete putrefaction of a corpse.

—Albert Wolff, critic

REYNOLDS, SIR JOSHUA

1723-1792, painter

I consider Reynolds's *Discourses to the Royal Academy* as the Simulations of the Hypocrite who smiles particularly where he means to Betray.

—William Blake, poet

RIGGS, BOBBY

1918-   , U.S. tennis champion

He can't hear, can't see, walks like a duck and is an idiot besides.

—Rosemary Casals, female
tennis ace

ROBINSON, JACKIE

1919-   , baseball player

When Branch Rickey of the Dodgers decided Jackie Robinson was ready for the Dodgers with just one more year of seasoning with the Montreal Farm Club, Clay Hopper asked Rickey directly, "You don't really think Nigrahs are human beings, do you?" [Yet Hopper treated Robinson fairly as a player.]

—Clay Hopper, manager of
the Montreal Farm Club

ROCKWELL, NORMAN

1894-1979, artist

He knew he didn't portray America. He portrayed Americana. His boys were all Tom Sawyers, his doctors made house calls, and his dogs were puppies.

—Ellen Goodman, columnist

ROGERS, WILL (WILLIAM PENN ADAIR ROGERS)

1879-1935, comedian

The bosom friend of senators and congressmen was about as daring as an early Shirley Temple movie.

—James Thurber, author

RUSSELL, BILL

1934-   , basketball player

Coon! —Go back to Africa, you baboon! Black Nigger!

—Fans at St. Louis upon Russell's
first appearance with
the Boston Celtics

RUSSELL, LILLIAN

1861-1922, actress, entertainer

Artistically Lillian Russell added little to theatrical history except an aptitude for commercializing sex appeal, a process on which Hollywood would infinitely elaborate, and of course her amazing ability to hit high C eight times in a performance.

—John Burke, writer
on entertainment

SARGENT, JOHN SINGER

1856-1925, artist

It is positively dangerous to sit next to Sargent. It is taking your face in your hands.

—Anonymous

A sepulchre of dulness and propriety.

—James Abbott McNeill Whistler,
American painter and
etcher in England

SCOTT, SIR GEORGE GILBERT

1811-1878, architect

Gilbert Scott was the supreme model of a Samuel Smiles self-made man . . . with all the vigour and all the lack of subtlety that one would expect.

—R. Furneaux-Jordan, author

PETER SELLERS
1925-   , actor

On a promotional tour of her book *Sophia Loren: Living and Loving*, the actress was told that Peter Sellers, her co-star in *The Millionairess*, was not mentioned in the book as one of her lovers. "I only wrote about things that were important to me," she replied without batting an eye.

—*Time* magazine

STANFORD, SIR CHARLES VILLIERS
1852-1924, composer

The stuff I hate and which I know is ruining any chance for good music in England is stuff like Stanford's which is neither fish, flesh, fowl nor good red-herring.

—Edward Elgar, British composer

Stanford is all crotchets and fads and moods.

—Gustav Holst, English composer

STENGEL, CASEY
1891-   , baseball manager

He had two tempers: One for the public and writers, and one for the players under him. The players were frequently dressed down in the dugout and clubhouse. He could charm the shoes off of you, if he wanted to, but he could also be rough. And after the first couple of seasons, he began to believe he had as much "magic" as the newspapers said he did.

—Phil Rizzuto, New York Yankee
player and announcer

He remains a figure of romantic nostalgia for those with 19th-century dugout vision.

—Howard Cosell, sports announcer

SULLIVAN, SIR ARTHUR SEYMOUR
1842-1900, composer

He is like a man who sits on a stove and then complains that his backside is burning.

—W.S. Gilbert, British
playwright and poet

TRUMAN, MARGARET (MRS. CLIFTON DANIELS)
1924-   , daughter of U.S.
President Harry S Truman

Miss Truman is a unique American phenomenon with a pleasant voice of little size and fair quality . . . yet Miss Truman cannot sing very well. She is flat a good deal of the time . . . she communicates almost nothing of the music she presents . . . There are few moments during her recital when one can relax and feel confident that she will make her goal, which is the end of her song.

—Paul Hume, music critic,
Washington *Post*

VALENTINO, RUDOLPH
(RUDOLPHO DI VALENTINA D'AUTONGUOLIA)
1895-1926, actor

It's difficult to see today the magnetism that he evidently exerted; it has been said that he had the acting talents of the average wardrobe, and he certainly seemed to restrict his range to a great deal of eye rolling, eye-brow jerking and facial smouldering.

—Clyde Jeavons and Jeremy
Pascall, writers on film

WAGNER, RICHARD
1813-1883, German composer

Wagner's music is better than it sounds.

—Mark Twain, American
novelist and humorist

(On *Die Meistersinger*)
Of all the bête, clumsy, blundering, boggling, baboon-blooded stuff I ever saw on a human stage, that thing last night beat—as far as the story and acting went—and of all the affected, sapless, soulless, beginningless, endless, topless, bottomless, topsiturviest, tuneless, scrannelpipiest—tongs and boniest—doggerel of sounds I ever endured the deadliness of, that eternity of nothing was deadliest, as far as its sound went. I never was so relieved, so far as I can remember, in my life, by the stopping of any sound—not excepting railroad whistles—as I was by the cessation of the cobbler's bellowing.

—John Ruskin, English writer, art
critic, and social reformer

Is Wagner a human being at all? Is he not rather a disease?

—Friedrich Nietzsche, German
philosopher

Wagner is evidently mad.

—Hector Berlioz, French composer

Wagner has beautiful moments but awful quarter-hours.

—Giocchino Antonio Rossini,
Italian composer

WHISTLER, JAMES ABBOT McNEILL

1834-1903, American painter and etcher in England

For Mr. Whistler's own sake [one] ought not to have admitted works into the gallery in which the ill-educated conceit of the artist so nearly approached the aspect of wilful imposture. I have seen, and heard, much of Cockney impudence before now; but never expected to hear a coxcomb ask two hundred guineas for flinging a pot of paint in the public's face.

—John Ruskin, art critic
and writer

(On Whistler's "Symphony in Grey and Green")
I never saw anything so impudent on the walls of any exhibition, in any country, as last year in London. It was a daub professing to be a "harmony in pink and white" (or some such nonsense); absolute rubbish, and which had taken about a quarter of an hour to scrawl or daub—it had no pretence to be called painting. The price asked for it was two hundred and fifty guineas.

—John Ruskin

With our James vulgarity begins at home, and should be allowed to stay there.

—Oscar Wilde, British poet,
novelist, and dramatist

As for borrowing Mr. Whistler's ideas about art, the only thoroughly original ideas I have ever heard him express have had reference to his own superiority as a painter over painters greater than himself.

—Oscar Wilde

WILDE, OSCAR
1864-1900, British poet, novelist, and dramatist born in Ireland

What has Oscar in common with Art? Except that he dines at our tables and picks from our platters the plums for the pudding he peddles in the provinces. Oscar—the amiable, irresponsible, esurient Oscar—with no more sense of a picture than the fit of a coat, has the courage of the opinions of others.

—James Abbott McNeill Whistler,
American painter and etcher

Chapter Six
• • • •
PROFESSIONALS

Practitioners of all professions have been the recipients of insults, but none more so than doctors and lawyers. They are reputed to be downright disreputable, ineffective, incompetent, money-grabbing, and what not. Some claim doctors encourage unnecessary visits and operations. When their patients are ill, they are not present and their science is of no avail. They are more prompt in sending out bills than in responding to a cry for help. They are all quacks, so if the patient gets well, it was God's fine hand, not the doctor's.

Worse crimes yet have been imputed to lawyers, who *mis*-represent more than they represent, who keep half of what judgments they have secured for needy clients, who have studied the law in order to bypass it. They stand, therefore, more often on the side of the lawless than the lawful. They appear never to have heard of real justice.

But teachers and clergymen hardly have admirable reputations: they are said to be dull, soporific, even hypocritical, considering the frequent discrepancy between their words and deeds. Of generals and lesser officers, it is said that they fight wars well—but from a safe distance and in comfort.

All these reputations and distortions are reflected in the pages that follow.

ALLEN, WILLIAM
1770-1843, philanthropist

All the world is a little queer save thee and me, and even thou art a little queer.
> —Robert Owen, attributed,
> American social reformer

ARNOLD, BENEDICT
1741-1801, Revolutionary soldier who became a traitor

With Benedict Arnold honor was not a character neatly defined or conveniently abstract, as with most of us. It was his peace of mind, it was his sense of superiority over other men. It was his instinct to command, and when he felt that it was not respected he was hostile or aloof. He was the world in terms of this domineering self. When he embraced a cause he did so vigorously, whole-heartedly, with no sense of duty or submission to a higher self, higher than his personal ambition.
> —Charles Coleman Sellers, author

From some traits of his character which have lately come to my knowledge, he seems to have been so hackneyed in villainy, and so lost to all sense of honor and shame that while his facilities will enable him to continue his sordid pursuits there will be no time for remorse.

—George Washington, U.S. president

ARNOLD, THOMAS
1795-1842, headmaster

Despite his high seriousness, Arnold had never gone through the process of growing up. At the age of ten he was already as great a prig as during his headmastership.

—Michael Holroyd, author

ATTERBURY, FRANCIS
1662-1732, Bishop of Rochester

Atterbury goes before, and sets everything on fire. I come after him with a bucket of water.

—George Smalridge

. . . a mind inexhaustibly rich in all the resources of controversy, and familiar with all the artifices which make falsehood look like truth and ignorance like knowledge.

—T.B. Macaulay, British historian,
essayist, poet, and statesman

BEECHER, HENRY WARD
1813-1887, American preacher and lecturer

A dunghill covered with flowers.

—Henry Watterson, American
journalist

Mankind fell in Adam, and has been falling ever since, but never touched bottom till it got to Henry Ward Beecher.

> --Tom Appleton, American
> essayist, poet, and artist

In Boston the human race is divided into 'the Good, the Bad, and the Beechers.'

> —W.M. Taylor, clergyman

He came out for the right side of every question—always a little too late.

> —Sinclair Lewis, author

The Reverend Henry Ward Beecher
Called a hen a most elegant creature.
   The hen, pleased with that,
    Laid two eggs in his hat.
And thus did the hen reward Beecher.

> —Oliver Wendell Holmes,
> writer and jurist

BERKELEY, GEORGE

1685-1753, philosopher and clergyman

And *God*-appointed Berkeley that proved
   all things a dream,
That this pragmatical, preposterous pig
   Of a world, its farrow
   that so solid seem,
Must vanish on the instant if the mind
   But change its theme.

> —William Butler Yeats, poet
> and playwright

BEVAN, ANEURIN
1897-1960, British political leader

He enjoys prophesying the imminent fall of the capitalist system and is prepared to play a part, any part, in its burial —except that of a mute.

—Harold Macmillan, British
prime minister

BROUGHAM, HENRY PETER, LORD
1778-1868, lawyer, critic, statesman, author

When Lord Brougham, a lawyer of uncertain reputation, appeared at a theatre performance, Sydney Smith said audibly: Here comes counsel for the other side.

—Sydney Smith, British clergy-
and writer, and wit

BROWNE, SIR THOMAS
1605-1682, physician, author

Lord, deliver me from myself.

—On himself

BRYAN, WILLIAM JENNINGS
1860-1925, American statesman and lawyer

Has it been duly marked by historians that William Jennings Bryan's last secular act on this globe of sin was to catch flies?

—H.L. Mencken, American Writer, editor, and
critic; in an obituary, Bryan having died
only weeks after the Stokes trial

BUTLER, BENJAMIN FRANKLIN
1818-1893, American soldier

The only wonder is that a character so foolish, so grovelling and obscene, can for a moment be admitted into decent society anywhere out of the pale of prostitutes and debauchees.

—Anonymous

A man whom all the waters of Massachusetts Bay cannot wash back into decency.

—Anonymous

If there comes a time when there is an absolute dearth of news, when you can't think of anything to make an interesting letter, there is always one thing you can do, and that is to pitch into Ben Butler.

—Murat Halstead, journalist

BUTLER, NICHOLAS MURRAY
1862-1947, American educator, scholar

His conceit is consummate .. He has the bearing of a Roman emperor and he honestly believes that he was born to lead if not to rule.

—Dorothy Dunbar Bromley,
American author

As the self-appointed intellectual leader of the American plutocracy, he now calms the fears of the wealthy, now chides them gently when he wishes to do a little discreet begging for Columbia University.

—Dorothy Dunbar Bromley

CHASE, SAMUEL

1741-1811, Associate Justice, U.S. Supreme Court

> Cursed of thy father, scum of all that's base,
> Thy sight is odious, and thy name is . . . [Chase].
>
> —Philadelphia *Aurora*

CUSHING, RICHARD CARDINAL

1895-1970, Roman Catholic clergyman

Richard Cardinal Cushing today accepted an invitation to deliver the invocation at the inauguration of Saint John Kennedy as President of the United States.

—*Boston Globe*

DARROW, CLARENCE

1857-1938, lawyer

Nobody in the world was ever more adept in convincing twelve men that another man who had bombed somebody, or poisoned somebody, or . . . with psychopathic urge, taken a little boy into the Michigan dunes and beaten the life out of him, hadn't either bombed, or poisoned or . . . beaten anybody . . . It's a great gift.

—General Hugh S. Johnson, New
Deal chieftain in report to FDR

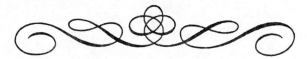

DECATUR, STEPHEN

1779-1820, American naval officer

In answer to Decatur's immortal toast of April 1816: Our country!, In her intercourse with foreign nations may she always be in the right; but our country right or wrong! The assertion "My country right or wrong" is like saying, "My mother drunk or sober."

—G.K. Chesterton, British writer

DEPEW, CHAUNCEY MITCHELL

1834-1928, lawyer, politician

I am reminded of Chauncey Depew, who said to the equally obese William Howard Taft at a dinner before the latter became President. "I hope, if it is a girl, Mr. Taft will name it for his charming wife." To which Taft responded, "If it is a girl, I shall, of course name it for my lovely helpmate of many years. And if it is a boy, I shall claim the father's prerogative and name it Junior. But, if as I suspect, it is only a bag of wind, I shall name it Chauncey Depew."

—Robert Kerr, U.S. senator

Dr. Depew says that if you open my mouth and drop in a dinner, up will come a speech. But I warn you that if you open your mouths and drop in one of Mr. Depew's speeches, up will come your dinners.

—Joseph H. Choate, American
lawyer and diplomat

DEWEY, JOHN
1859-1952, philosopher, pedagogue

In the bedlam of tragedy, melodrama and light opera in which we live, Dewey is still the master of the commonplace.

—C.E. Ayres

Not only is his own style dull, but his dullness infects everybody who has anything to write about his theories of education.

—Max Eastman, American author

DEWEY, THOMAS EDMUND
1902-1971, lawyer, politician

He is just about the nastiest little man I've ever known. He struts sitting down.

—Mrs. Clarence Dykstra, wife of
American educator and
civic admininstrator

Dewey, cool, cold, low-voiced, was like a softly growling bull terrier willing to take on all comers if he could get in one good bite.

—Edwin C. Hill, author

Dewey has thrown his diaper in the ring.

—Harold Ickes, American statesman

DULLES, JOHN FOSTER

1888-1959, lawyer, U.S. secretary of state

As Secretary, he lived, acted, spoke, reacted, advanced, retreated, threatened, courted, summarized, analysed, briefed, cross-examined, responded, appealed objected, thrust, parried—like a lawyer.

—Emmet John Hughes, author
and journalist

Smooth is an inadequate word for Dulles. His prevarications are so highly polished as to be aesthetically pleasurable.

—I.F. Stone, commentator
and editor-publisher

EDDY, MARY MORSE BAKER GLOVER PATTERSON

1821-1910, founder of the Church of Christ, Scientist

What she has really "discovered" are ways and means of perverting and prostituting the science of healing to her own ecclesiastical aggrandizement, and to the moral and physical depravity of her dupes.

—Mrs. Josephine Curtis Woodbury

. . . a brass god with clay legs.

—Mark Twain, American
novelist and humorist

FISHER, JOHN ARBUTHNOT, LORD FISHER OF KILVERSTONE
1841-1920, Admiral of the Fleet

He was a mixture of Macchiavelli and child, which must have been extraordinarily baffling to politicians and men of the world.

—Esther Meynell

FISK, JAMES, JR.
1834-1872, financier

. . . the glaring meteor, abominable in his lusts, and flagrant in his violation of public decency. . .

—Henry Ward Beecher, American preacher, orator, and lecturer

FLETCHER, STEPHEN
(n.d), bookseller

He was a very proud, confident, ill-natured, impudent, ignorant fellow, peevish and forward to his wife (whom he used to beat), a great sot, and whoring prostituted wretch, and of no credit.

—Thomas Hearne, antiquarian and diarist

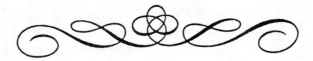

FORD, HENRY
1863-1947, industrialist

If only Ford himself were properly assembled!
If only he would do in himself what he has done in his factory!

—Samuel S. Marquess, author

The ordinary mortal is content to hitch his wagon to a star. This is a sport too tame for Henry Ford. He prefers to hang on to the tail of a comet. It is less conventional, more spectacular and furnishes more thrills.

—Samuel S. Marquess

GARDINER, STEPHEN
1483-1555, Bishop of Winchester

I will not here speak of that which hath been constantly reported to me touching the monstrous making and misshaped fashion of his feet and toes, and the nails whereof were said not to be like to other men's, but to crook downwards, and to be sharp like the Claws of ravening Beasts.

—John Roxe, English clergyman
and author

GENERAL MOTORS

I've always thought that C.E. Wilson [President of G.M.] was really a very decent, genuine human beingg. The test of that is whether you can still act human after going through the GM Corporation machine, and he passed that test.

—Walther Reuther, UAW leader

GOMPERS, SAMUEL
1850-1924, American labor leader

Had Mr. Gompers been able to add six inches to his height, he would have been one of our great tragedians.

—John Frey, union leader

Like a piece of worn-out buffalo robe which has lain in the garret and been chewed by the moths since 1890, and then been thrown out in the rain and laid in the gutter for a year or two, and then been dragged by a puppy dog to cut his teeth on.

—Mark Sullivan, critic of American culture, describing Gompers' hair

GRAY, L. PATRICK
1920-   , FBI director

He's a big clown.

—Richard M. Nixon, U.S. president

HAIG, DOUGLAS, EARL
1861-1928, soldier

With the publication of his Private Papers in 1952, he committed suicide 25 years after his death.

—Lord Beaverbrook, British newspaper publisher and statesman

What a rascal Haig was. One of the biggest rascals in a long time. Twisting, turning, conspiring against French, pushing him out, conniving with the King. Oh, he is a disgraceful story.

—Lord Beaverbrook

Haig was devoid of the gift of intelligible and coherent expression.

—David Lloyd George,
British prime minister

HALLECK, HENRY WAGER
1815-1872, soldier, administrator

Originates nothing, anticipates nothing, takes no responsibility, plans nothing, suggests nothing, is good for nothing.

—Gideon Welles, American statesman

HARRIS, LOU
1921-   , political pollster

Old Lou is full of shit on this one.

—John F. Kennedy, U.S. president, on a
prediction that the 1964 New York
gubernatorial race would be close.
Rockefeller won by 16 percent.

HARVEY, GABRIEL
1545-1630, lawyer and translator

This dodipoule, this didopper . . . Why, thou arrant butter whore, thou cosqueane & scrattop of scoldes, wilt thou never leave afflicting a dead Carcasse . . . a wispe, a wispe, jippe, rippe, you kitchin-stuff wranger.

—Thomas Nashe, author and satirist

HENDERSON, ARTHUR
1863-1935, labor leader, statesman

We will support Henderson as a rope supports a man who is hanged.

—V.I. Lenin, Soviet Communist leader

HOOVER, J(OHN) EDGAR
1895-1972, first director of the FBI

He never read anything that would broaden his mind or give depth to his thinking. I never knew him to have an intellectual or educated friend.

—William Sullivan, high-ranking
FBI official

Hoover walks with a rather mincing step, almost feminine. This gait may be a relic of his valedictorian days, for at all times he appears to be making his way as though the caution of a teacher not to race to the rostrum was ringing in his ears.

—Walter Trohan

I'd rather have him inside the tent pissing out, than outside pissing in.

—Lyndon B. Johnson, U.S. president

HUGHES, HOWARD ROBARD
1905-1976, film maker, industrialist, inventor

The spook of American Capitalism .. suspicious and withdrawn, elusive to the point of being almost invisible, he is loath to give anything up, loath to admit error . . . There is one aspect of his character about which his former associates are agreed: he abhors making a decision.

—*Fortune* magazine; cited in
Elaine Davenport and Paul
Eddy with Mark Hurwitz,
The Hughes Papers

Hughes was the only man I ever knew who had to die to prove he had been alive.

—Walter Kane

HUME, DAVID
1711-1776, philosopher, historian

Hume is always idiomatic, but his idioms are constantly wrong.

—Walter Bagehot, British
social scientist

His face was broad and flat, his mouth wide, and without any other expression than that of imbecility. His eyes were vacant and spiritless, and the corpusculence of his whole person was far better fitted to communicate the idea of a turtle-eating Alderman, than of a refined philosopher.

—James Caulfield, Earl of
Charlemont, statesman

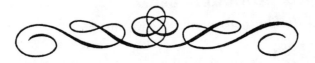

JARRELL, RANDALL
1914-1965, educator, author

He was bearded, formidable, bristling, with a high-pitched nervous voice and the wariness of a porcupine.

—Stanely Kunitz, American
writer and editor

JAY, JOHN
1745-1829, jurist, statesman, diplomat

Damn John Jay! Damn every one that won't damn John Jay! Damn every one that won't put lights in his windows and sit up all night damning John Jay!!!

—Anonymous

KNOX, JOHN
1505-1572, Scottish reformer

One is tempted almost to say that there was more of Jesus in St. Theresa's little finger than in John Knox's whole body.

—Matthew Arnold, English
poet, critic, and essayist

LIVINGSTONE, EDWARD
1898-1967, publisher

He really thought there was nothing he could not do, so he often did it.

—Archibald MacLeish, American poet

MacARTHUR, DOUGLAS
1880-1964, American General of the Army

I fired him because he wouldn't respect the authority of the President. That's the answer to that. I didn't fire him because he was a dumb son-of-a-bitch, although he was, but that's not against the law for generals. If it was, half to three quarters of them would be in jail.

—Harry S Truman, U.S. president

Oh yes, I studied dramatics under him for twelve years.

—Dwight D. Eisenhower, U.S. president

MARSHALL, JOHN
1755-1835, Chief Justice of the U.S. Supreme Court

[The] crafty chief judge [whose] twistifications [of the law showed his hatred of] the government of his country.

—Thomas Jefferson, U.S. president

MAYER, LOUIS BURT
1885-1957, motion picture producer

The reason so many people showed up at his funeral was because they wanted to make sure he was dead.

—Samuel Goldwyn, American
film producer

McCLELLAN, GEORGE B.

1826-1885, Union General in the American Civil War

I have just read your despatch about sore-tongued and fatigued horses. Will you pardon me for asking what the horses of your army have done since the battle of Antietam that fatigues anything?

—Abraham Lincoln, U.S. president

My dear McClellan: If you don't want to use the army, I should like to borrow it for a while. Yours respectfully, A. Lincoln.

—Abraham Lincoln

[McClellan] is an admirable Engineer, but he seems to have a special talent for the stationary engine.

—Abraham Lincoln

McLAUGHLIN, JOHN

(n.d.), clergyman

To build an "ethical stone wall" around President Nixon at this point would require a Merlin of a stonemason. Father John McLaughlin is merely an apprentice bricklayer with a forked tongue for a trowel and hot air for mortar.

—*Newsweek* magazine

McPHERSON, AIMEE SEMPLE

1890-1944, evangelist

Mrs. McPherson has the nerve of a brass monkey and the philosophy of the Midway—"Never give a sucker an even break"—is grounded in her.

—Morrow Mayo

NAPIER, SIR CHARLES JAMES
1782-1853, soldier, administrator

Napier Singh was a lion indeed . . . But this lion, though the bravest of animals, was the most quarrelsome that ever lashed a tail and roared in a jungle.

—William Makepeace Thackeray, author

NEWMAN, JOHN HENRY, CARDINAL
1801-1890, theologian

To me he seems to have been the most artificial man of our generation, full of ecclesiastical loves and hatred.

—Benjamin Jowett, English educator
and Greek scholar

Poor Newman! He was a great hater!

—Henry Edward Manning, cardinal
of the Roman Catholic Church

PIKE, ZEBULON MONTGOMERY
1779-1813, soldier, explorer

Pike's name remains perpetuated in a great natural monument more than 14,000 feet in height, an honour totally unjustified and totally undeserved.

—John Terrell, author

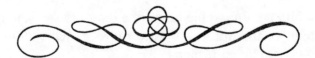

PRIESTLEY, JOSEPH

1733-1804, theologian, man of science

Of Dr. Priestley's theological works, he [Samuel Johnson] remarked, that they tend to unsettle everything and yet settled nothing.

—James Boswell, author

He is one of the most voluminous writers of any age or country, and probably he is of all voluminous writers the one who has the fewest readers.

—Henry, Lord Brougham,
British statesman

PYM, JOHN

1584-1643, British parliamentarian

The most popular man, and the most able to do hurte, that hath lived in any tyme.

—Edward Hyde, Earl of Clarendon

RALEIGH, SIR WALTER

1552-1618, officer, historian, poet, courtier

I will prove you the mororiousest traitor that ever came to the bar . . . thou art a monster; thou hast an English face, but a Spanish heart. Thou art the most vile and execrable Traitor that ever lived . . . I want words sufficient to express thy viperous Treasons . . . Thou art an odious fellow, thy name is hateful to all the realm of England . . . There never lived a viler viper upon the face of the earth than thou.

—Sir Edward Coke, judge and jurist

REUTHER, WALTER PHILIP
1907-1970 labor leader

It's hard to guess where Walter's ideas come from. If you have an idea that is worth anything, you might as well give it to him because if you don't he'll steal it from you.

—Anonymous

Walter Reuther is the most dangerous man in Detroit because no one is more skillful at bringing about revolution without seeming to disturb the existing forms of society.

—George Romney, president
of American Motors

. . . a labor leader turned radical political . . . I can think of nothing more detrimental to this nation than for any President to owe his election to, and thereby be a captive of, a political boss like Walter Reuther.

—Richard M. Nixon, U.S. president

ROCKEFELLER, JOHN DAVISON
1839-1937, industrialist, philanthropist

Rockefeller made his money in oil, which he discovered at the bottom of wells. Oil was crude in those days, but so was Rockefeller. Now both are considered quite refined.

—Richard Armour, author

John D. Rockefeller can be fully described as a man made in the image of the ideal money-maker . . . An ideal money-maker is a machine the details of which are diagrammed on the asbestos blueprints which paper the walls of hell.

—Thomas Lawson, American stock-
market speculator and author

No candid study of his career can lead to other conclusion than that he is a victim of perhaps the ugliest . . . of all passions, that for money, money as an end . . .

It is not a pleasant picture . . . this money-maniac secretly, patiently, eternally plotting how he may add to his wealth. Nor is the man himself pleasanter to look upon . . . portraits show . . . craftiness, cruelty, and something indefinably repulsive . . .

—Ida M. Tarbell, American author

There was a time, I am told on good authority, when John D. Rockefeller was getting one million dollars a day; and still, I have reason to believe, they buried him in a pair of pants.

—Milton Mayer, American author

ROHAYTAN, FELIX
(n.d.), financial advisor

He has to have his place in the sun, which is understandable—but all day long!

—Edward Koch, mayor of
New York City

ROYCE, JOSIAH
1855-1916, philosopher, teacher

There was a suggestion about him of the benevolent ogre or the old child, in whom a preternatural sharpness of insight lurked beneath a grotesque mask.

—George Santayana, American
philosopher and poet

RUSH, RICHARD

1780-1850, American lawyer, statesman, diplomat

Never was ability so much below mediocrity so well rewarded; no, not even when Caligula's horse was made a consul.

—John Randolph, American
statesman and orator

RUSSELL, BERTRAND ARTHUR WILLIAM, THIRD EARL

1873-1970, philosopher

The enemy of all mankind, you are, full of the lust of enmity. It is *not* the hatred of falsehood which inspires you. It is the hatred of people, of flesh and blood. It is a perverted, mental blood-lust. Why don't you own it?

—D.H. Lawrence, author

He only feels life through his brain, or through sex, and there is a gulf between these two separate departments.

—Lady Ottoline Morrell

SHERIDAN, PHILIP HENRY

1831-1888, American soldier

The general is a stumpy, quadrangular little man, with a forehead of no promise and hair so short that it looks like a coat of black paint.

—George Templeton Strong, lawyer

ST. CLAIR, JAMES

1920-   , Watergate lawyer for Nixon

The trouble with St. Clair is that he is all case and no cause.

—William Sloan Coffin, clergyman

He is the 1970s version of the guy whom the sodbusters hired when the cattlemen tried to tear down their fences in the 1880s—a hired gun.

—George V. Higgins, lawyer-author

WHITEFIELD, GEORGE

1714-1770, leader of the Calvinistic Methodist Church

I heard him once, and it was as low, confused, puerile, conceited, ill-natured, enthusiastic a performance as I ever heard.

—Jonathan Mayhew, clergyman

WILMOT, JOHN, EARL OF ROCHESTER

1647-1680, poet, libertine

Mean in each action, lewd in every limb
Manners themselves are mischievous in him.

—John Sheffield, Earl of Mulgrave

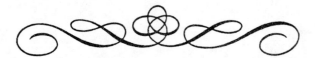

WITTGENSTEIN, LUDWIG JOSEF JOHANN
1889-1951, philosopher

My German engineer, I think, is a fool. He thinks nothing empirical is knowable—I asked him to admit that there was not a rhinoceros in the room, but he wouldn't.

—Bertrand Russell, British
philosopher

Chapter Seven

• • • •

SUNDRY DEPRECATIONS

ART AND ARTISTS

We now live in the Era of Incompetence; we have painters who can't paint, poets who can't rhyme and composers
who whistle dissonance.

—Dagobert D. Runes, philosopher
and publisher

The only thing wrong with architecture is architects.

—Frank Lloyd Wright, architect

A highbrow is the kind of person who looks at a sausage
and thinks of Picasso.

—A.P. Herbert. British author
and member of Parliament

Abstract art? A product of the untalented, sold by the unprincipled to the utterly bewildered.

—Al Capp, cartoonist
and humorist

[Painting is] the art of protecting flat surfaces from the weather and exposing them to the critic.

—Ambrose Bierce, writer

The true artist will let his wife starve, his children go barefoot, his mother drudge for his living at seventy, sooner than work at anything but his art.

—G.B. Shaw, dramatist and critic

BUSINESS AND FINANCE

The nature of business is swindling.

—August Bebel, German
socialist and author

All business sagacity reduces itself in the last analysis to a judicious use of sabotage.

—Thorstein Veblen, political economist, author, and educator

Merchandising being the most subtile searcher after hidden gain, the most covetous devourer of her detected prey, is never happy in enjoyment, but always most miserably tormented with the desire of more . . . Thus the trades of merchandising [and] bankers, are both necessary, profitable, and laborious; and yet they are . . . illiberal, sordid, and base ways of getting, because they are not arts but laborious cheats . . . which is the . . . trade not of a . . . well-meaning . . . just good man, but of a crafty, close deceitful knavish dealer . . . [Among such men] lying, imposing, cheating and perjury is most frequent; neither is there any way of achieving profit which they think disdainful . . . For no men grow rich without deceit. . . .

—Henry Morton Robinson, novelist

Businessmen who would blush to be seen in a five-year-old car proudly make medieval pronouncements on economics.

—Henry Morton Robinson

I don't have a whole lot of faith in what the oil companies say.

—Jay Rockefeller, governor of West Virginia and great-grandson of John D., founder of Standard Oil

A corporation cannot blush. It is a body, it is true; has certainly a head—a new one each year; arms it has and very long ones, for it can reach anything; a throat to swallow the rights of the community, and a stomach to digest them! But who ever yet discovered in the anatomy of any corporation, either bowels or a heart?

—Howel Walsh

An excellent monument might be erected to the unknown stockholder. It might take the form of a solid stone arc of faith apparently floating in a pool of water.

—Felix Riesenberg, mariner and author

There is an amazing amount of mediocrity even among top businessmen. I know, I've seen them; 90 percent of them are mediocre, pompous, narrow, stupid, neanderthal. . .

—John R. Connally, politician

A bank is the thing that will always lend you money if you can prove you don't need it.

—Joe E. Lewis, comedian

I must atone for my wealth.

—Otto Kahn, industrialist

I regard my employees as I do a machine, to be used to my advantage, and when they are old and of no further use, I cast them into the street.

—a manufacturer to Samuel
Gompers, labor leader

The Almighty Dollar, the great object of universal devotion throughout the land.

—Washington Irving, author

I've labored long and hard for bread—
For honor and for riches—
But on my corns too long you've tred,
You fine-haired sons of bitches.

—Black Bart, stagecoach robber

My father always told me that all businessmen were sons of bitches, but I never believed it till now.

—John F. Kennedy, U.S. president
during U.S. Steel crisis, reported
by Wallace Carroll in the *New
York Times*, April 23, 1962

I said sons of bitches, bastards, or pricks. I don't know which. But I never said anything about *all* businessmen.

—John F. Kennedy, concerning
the above

BUREAUCRACY AND INEFFICIENCY

The only thing that saves us from the bureaucracy is inefficiency. An efficient bureaucracy is the greatest threat to liberty.

—Eugene McCarthy, U.S. senator

All my life I've known better than to depend on the experts. How could I have been so stupid, to let them go ahead?

—John F. Kennedy, U.S. president,
after the 1961 Bay of Pigs crisis

CONGRESS

Fleas can be taught nearly anything that a congressman can.

—Mark Twain, novelist and humorist

Suppose you were an idiot, and suppose you were a member of Congress; but I repeat myself.

—Mark Twain

Some statesmen go to Congress and some go to hell. It is the same thing, after all.

—Eugene Field, poet and journalist

We've had plenty of congressmen who ended up in jail. What's wrong with one who started in jail?

—Melvin Perkins, congressional candidate, incarcerated for assaulting a woman bus driver

The Senate passed a bill appropriating $15 million for food, but the House of Representatives has not approved it. They must think it would encourage hunger.

—Will Rogers, journalist

CULTURE AND CIVILIZATION

Three millions yearly for manure.
But not one cent for literature.

—Ellis Parker Butler

History is bunk.

—Henry Ford, industrialist

The Ku Klux Klan has been the vulture of America for almost a century . . . It is one enemy that has engaged in continual warfare against America since the Civil War. Its ally is hatred. Its weapon is terror. And its aim is the destruction of our democracy . . The Klan runs like a bloody thread through the noose every subversive outfit was eager to wrap around America's neck.

—Walter Winchell, columnist

America is so terribly grim in spite of all that material prosperity. They no longer know how to weep. Compassion and the old neighborliness have gone; people stand by and do nothing when friends and neighbors are attacked, libeled and ruined. The worst thing is what it has done to the children. They are being taught to admire and emulate stool pidgeons, to betray and to hate, and all in a sickening atmosphere of religious hypocrisy.

—Charlie Chaplin, actor,
on the FBI and IRS

From every Englishman emanates a kind of gas,
The deadly choke-damp of boredom.

—Heinrich Heine, author

For him Art has no marvel, and Beauty no meaning, and the Past no message.

—Oscar Wilde, author, talking
about the average American

The atomic secret is the fruit of your sick imaginations: Science develops everywhere at the same rhythm, and the manufacture of bombs is a mere matter of industrial capacities.

—Jean-Paul Sartre, philosopher,
addressing Americans

I have seen the best minds of my generation destroyed by madness.

—Allen Ginsberg, poet

The thing that impresses me most about America is the way parents obey their children.

—Duke of Windsor

Sometimes, if we have an evening at home, we're likely to sit here with a tray and watch straight through, like Mr. Average Man, all the dumb television shows.

—Betsy Cronkite, wife of television
newsman Walter Cronkite

DOCTORS AND PATIENTS

In regard to the fascinating subject of my operation, I should naturally like to go on for several pages . . . but will confine myself to saying that I think the doc should have read just one book before picking up the saw.

—John F. Kennedy, U.S. president

Doctors think a lot of patients are cured who have simply quit in disgust.

—Don Herold, writer and artist

Doctors are men who prescribe medicines of which they know little, to cure diseases of which they know less, in human beings of whom they know nothing.

—Voltaire, satirist, philosopher,
dramatist, and historian

It was difficult for the Angel of Death to kill everybody in the whole world, so he appointed doctors to assist him.

—Nahman of Bratzlav, Jewish mystic

Witch doctors are as important as psychiatrists.

—T. Adeoye Lambe, physician

God Heals, and the doctor takes the fee.

—Benjamin Franklin, American
statesman and scientist

ON DOGMATISM AND DETERMINATION

The dogmas of the quiet past are inadequate to the stormy present.

—Abraham Lincoln, U.S. president

Of all heresies,
Orthodoxy is the deadliest.

—Chayym Zeldis, author

The Ku Klux Klan never dies. They just stop wearing sheets because sheets cost too much.

—Thurgood Marshall, U.S.
Supreme Court Justice

. . . people like a scrapper. I always try to be good-natured, but I certainly punch hell out of a lot of people.

—Wayne Lyman Morse,
U.S. senator

May the fleas of a thousand camels infest your armpits.

—Arab insult

Come on, you rascals, you bloody backs, you lobster scoundrels, fire if you dare, God damn you, fire and be damned, we know you dare not.

—Captain Thomas Preston, to the mob
at the 1770 Boston Massacre

A radical is a man with both feet firmly placed in the air.

—Franklin D. Roosevelt,
U.S. president

EDUCATION AND EDUCATORS

A professor is one who talks in someone else's sleep.

—W.H. Auden, poet

Our American professors like their literature clear and cold and pure and very dead.

—Sinclair Lewis, novelist

A professor is a man whose job it is to tell students how to solve the problems of life which he himself has tried to avoid by becoming a professor.

—Anonymous

Public schools . . . are becoming a nuisance, a pest, an abomination; and it is fit that the eyes and noses of mankind should, if posssible, be open to perceive it.

—William Cowper, poet

A lecturer is one with his hand in your pocket, his tongue in your ear, and his faith in your patience.

—Ambrose Bierce, writer

He who can, does. He who cannot, teaches.

—G.B. Shaw, dramatist
and critic

Arrogance, pedantry, and dogmatism are the occupational diseases of those who spend their lives directing the intellects of the young.

—Henry Canby, writer,
teacher, and editor

Teaching is the last refuge of feeble minds with classical education.

—Aldous Huxley, novelist,
poet, and essayist

A Harvard professor is an educator who thinks the American eagle has two left wings.

—John M. Ashbrook,
U.S. Representative

ENTERTAINERS AND ENTERTAINMENT

[Acting is] the lowest of the arts, if an art at all, and [makes] slender demands on the intelligence of the individual exercising it. You can teach a child to act, but you can teach no child to paint pictures, or model statues, or to write prose.

—George Moore, novelist

[An actor] has delusions of adequacy.

—Walter Kerr, drama critic
and playwright

The scenery was beautiful but the actors got in front of it. The play left a taste of lukewarm parsnip juice.

—Alexander Woollcott,
critic and humorist

Perfectly Scandalous was one of those plays in which all of the actors unfortunately enunciated very clearly.

—Robert Benchley, humorist

Politics is developing more comedians than radio ever did.

—Jimmy Durante, comedian

Radio—the triumph of illiteracy.

—John Dos Passos, novelist

You can seduce a man's wife here, attack his daughter and wipe your hands on his canary bird, but if you don't like his movie, you're dead.

—Josef von Sternberg, film director

On ship they call them barnacles; in radio they attach themselves to desks and are called vice-presidents.

—Fred Allen, comedian

The Theatres—those Cages of Uncleanness, and publick Schools of Debauchery.

—St. Augustine, Church Father

Don't put your daughter on the stage, Mrs. Worthington.

—Noel Coward, dramatist, novelist, humorist, and actor

[Theater] is a most unholy trade.

—Henry James, novelist and critic

There is a total extinction of all taste: our authors are vulgar, gross, illiberal; the theatre swarms with wretched translations, and balled operas, and we have nothing new but improving abuse.

—Horace Walpole, author

Actors are a nuisance in the earth, the very offal of society.

—Timothy Dwight, clergyman, author, and editor

In the old days an actress tried to become a star. Today we have stars trying to be actresses.

—Sir Laurence Olivier, actor

That popular Stage-players (the very Pompes of the Dievell which we renounced in Baptisme, if we believe the Fathers) are sinfull, heathenish, lewde, ungodly Spectacle and most pernicious Corruptions; condemned in all ages, as intolerable Mischiefes to Churches, to Republickes, to the manners, mindes, and soules of men. And that the Profession of Play-poets, of Stage-players; together with the penning, acting and frequenting of Stage-playes, are unlawfull, infamous and misbeseeming Christians.

—William Prynne, Puritan
controversialist and jurist

Some actors think they are elevating the stage when they're merely depressing the audience.

—George A. Posne

You can pick out actors by the glazed look that comes into their eyes when the conversation wanders away from themselves.

—Michael Wilding, actor

GEOGRAPHIC RIVALRIES AND DEPRECATIONS

I heard one Californian say in mild disgust, "If we came out against smallpox, Arizona would be for it."

—John Gunther, author

It is hereby earnestly proposed that the U.S.A. would be much better off if that big, sprawling, incoherent, shapeless, slobbering civic idiot in the family of American communities, the City of Los Angeles, could be declared incompetent and placed in charge of a guardian like any individual mental defective.

—Westbrook Pegler, journalist

The only way to avoid Hollywood is to live there.

—Igor Stravinsky, composer
and conductor

I guess Hollywood won't consider me anything except a cold hunk of potato until I divorce my husband, give my baby away, and get my name and photograph in all the newspapers.

> —Maureen O'Hara, actress, as quoted
> by Hedda Hopper, movie critic

Sometimes Washington goes crazy, but then a democracy ought to fumble and flounder every once in a while—that's what democracy is.

> —Henry Kaiser, industrialist

Oklahoma is to sociology what Australia is to zoology. It is the place where the trials and errors of men, instead of nature, have been made only yesterday, and the results are as egregious as a duckbill or kangaroo. Oklahoma is full of manmade contradictions, perversities, and monstrosities.

> —George Milburn, author

Thought is barred in this city of Dreadful Joy [Los Angeles] and conversation is unknown.

> —Aldous Huxley, novelist
> and essayist

Los Angeles has of course been called every name in the book, from "nineteen suburbs in search of a metropolis" to a "circus without a tent" to "less a city than a perpetual convention."

> —Frank Lloyd Wright, architect

If you tilt the whole country sideways, Los Angeles is the place where everything loose will fall.

> —Daniel Webster, statesman
> and orator

What can we do with the western coast, a coast of 3,000 miles, rockbound, cheerless, uninviting, and not a harbor on it? What use have we for such a country? I will never vote one cent from the public treasury to place the Pacific Ocean one inch nearer Boston than it is now!

—Daniel Webster, statesman
and orator

I view great cities as pestilential to the morals, the health, and the liberties of man.

—Thomas Jefferson, U.S. president

This state [Colorado] has more sunshine and more bastards than any place on earth!

—from a statement of a convicted executive about Judge Ben Lindsey

A part of hell with the fires burnt out.

—General Custer, on South Dakota

Kansas had better stop raising corn and begin raising Hell.

—Mary Elizabeth Lease, lecturer
and writer

Kansas used to believe in Populism and free silver. It now believes in hot summers and a hot hereafter.

—Julian Street, author

There is no peace in Chicago. It is a city of terror and light, untamed.

—W.L. George

Having seen it [Chicago], I urgently desire never to see it again. It is inhabited by savages. Its air is dirt.

—Rudyard Kipling, author

New England is a . . . . house divided against itself.

—Howard Mumford Jones, writer

Bright and fierce and fickle is the South.

—Alfred Lord Tennyson, poet

The South, the poor South!

—Last words of John C. Calhoun, historian

Only Bostonians can understand Bostonians and thoroughly sympathize with the inconsequences of the Boston mind.

—Henry Adams, historian

Well, little old Noisyville-on the-Subway is good enough for me.

—O. Henry, author, on
New York City

The city like a ragged purple dream, the wonderful, cruel, enchanting, bewildering, fatal, great city.

—O. Henry, on New York City

Vulgar of manner, overfed,
Overdressed and underbred.

—Byron R. Newton, tax commissioner,
on New York City

Arkansas has its own popular motto and it is this: "I've never seen nothin', I don't know nothin', I hain't got nothin', and I don't want nothin'." . . . . It [Arkansas] just grew out of seepage.

—C.L. Edson, an Arkansas farmer

Come on, boys! We've got the damn Yankees on the run!

—General Wheeler

When asked whether Washingtonians in her opinion will like *Peter Pan*, in which she starred, Sandy Duncan responded in the affirmative: "I think they deal highly in fantasy here."

٥   ٥   ٥

Los Angeles is fertile soil for every kind of impostor that the face of the earth has been cursed by. The suckers all come sooner or later and the whole twelve months is open season.

—H.L. Mencken, quoting a local patriot

Let our workshops remain in Europe. The mobs of great cities add just so much to the support of pure government as sores do to the strength of the human body.

—Thomas Jefferson, U.S. president

LAWYERS AND THE LAW

The law is a ass.

—Charles Dickens, novelist

The laws I love; the lawyers I suspect.

—Charles Churchill,
poet and satirist

Whatever you do, never go to law; submit rather to almost any imposition; bear an oppression, rather than exhaust your spirits and your pocket in what is called a court of justice.

—Sir John Willis

A lawyer must first get on, then get honor, and then get honest.

Anonymous

A lawyer is a learned gentleman who rescues your estate from your enemies and keeps it himself.

—Anonymous

When there is a rift in the lute, the business of the lawyer is to widen the rift and gather the loot.

—Arthur Garfield Hays, lawyer

I think we may class the lawyer in the natural history of monsters.

—John Keats, poet

God works wonders now and then;
Behold! a lawyer, an honest man.

—Benjamin Franklin, statesman,
scientist, inventor, and writer

Sometimes a man who deserves to be looked down upon because he is a fool is despised only because he is a lawyer.

—C.L. Montesquieu, jurist
and philosophical writer

A man without money needs no more fear a crowd of lawyers than a crowd of pickpockets.

—William Wycherley, dramatist

Why, gentlemen, you cannot live without the lawyers, and certainly you cannot die without them.

> —Joseph H. Choate, lawyer
> and diplomat

Lawyer: One skilled in circumvention of the law.
Liar: A lawyer with a roving commission.

> —Ambrose Bierce, writer

Lawyers and physicians are an ill provision for any country.

> —Michel de Montaigne, essayist

LITERARY CRITICS AND CRITICISM

They who write ill, and they who ne'er durst write,
Turn critics out of mere revenge and spite.

> —John Dryden, poet,
> critic, and dramatist

The critic's symbol should be the tumble-bug; he deposits his egg in somebody else's dung, otherwise he could not hatch it.

> —Mark Twain, novelist
> and humorist

As for you, little envious Prigs, snarling bastards, puny Criticks, you'll soon have railed your last: Go hang yourselves!

> —François Rabelais, scholar
> and author

Thou eunuch of language . . . thou pimp of gender . . . murderous accoucheur of infant learning . . . thou pickle-herring in the puppet show of nonsense.

—Robert Burns, poet

Critics! Appalled, I venture on the name,
Those cut-throat bandits in the paths of fame.

—Robert Burns

Reviewers are usually people who would have been poets, historians, biographers, if they could: they have tried their talents at one or the other, and have failed; therefore turn critics.

—Samuel T. Coleridge,
poet and critic

Critics in general are venomous serpents that delight in hissing.

—W.B. Daniel

Animals are such agreeable friends—they ask no questions, they pass no criticism.

—George Eliot, novelist

What a blessed thing it is that nature, when she invented, manufactured, and patented her authors, contrived to make critics out of the chips that were left!

—Oliver Wendell Holmes,
writer and physician

A critic is a legless man who teaches running.

—Channing Pollack, playwright

A critic:
  A eunuch judging a man's lovemaking.
  A skydreaming eagle without wings.
  Pygmies with poison darts who live in
  The valley of the sleeping giants.
  —Dagobert D. Runes, philosophical
  writer and publisher

Pay no attention to what the critics say; here has never been set up a statue in honor of a critic.
  —Jan Sibelius, musician

Critics are like those of whom Demetrius declared that he took no more account of the wind that came from their mouths than of that which they expelled from their lower parts.
  —Leonardo da Vinci, painter, sculptor,
  musician, architect, scientist,
  and natural philosopher

I threw out several strident chapters. I no longer want to bark. But I hang onto my prejudices. They are the testicles of my mind.
  —Eric Hoffer, on his own
  writing efforts

All literary men are Red Sox fans. To be a Yankee fan in literary society is to endanger your life.
  —John Cheever, author

MILITARY MATTERS

A soldier is a slave—he does what he is told to do—everything is provided for him—his head is a superfluity. He is only a stick used by men to strike other men.

—Elbert Hubbard, writer

A modern general has said that that the best troops would be as follows: an Irishman half drunk, a Scotchman half starved, and an Englishman with his belly full.

—Caleb C. Colton, clergyman

A soldier is a man whose business it is to kill those who never offended him, and who are the innocent martyrs of other men's iniquities. Whatever may become of the abstract question of the justifiableness of war, it seems impossible that the soldier should not be a depraved and unnatural thing.

—William Godwin, philosopher
and writer

I do believe our army chaplains, taken as a class, are the worst men we have in the service.

—Abraham Lincoln, U.S. president

MODESTY

The less you speak of your greatness, the more I shall think of it. Mirrors are the accompaniments of dandies, not heroes. The men of history were not perpetually looking in the glass to make sure of their own size. They were absorbed in their work, and the world noticed what they accomplished.

—Francis Bacon, essayist, in
a reprimand to a friend

ON MUSIC AND MUSICIANS

There are no women composers, never have been, and possibly never will be.

—Sir Thomas Beecham, conductor

Music is but a fart that's sent
From the guts of an instrument.

—Anonymous

Hell is full of musical amateurs.

—G.B. Shaw, dramatist

Music is the brandy of the damned.

—G.B. Shaw

He was a fiddler, and consequently a rogue.

—Jonathan Swift, author

Jazz: Music invented for the torture of imbeciles.

—Henry van Dyke, poet,
writer, and diplomat

PERSONAL AFFRONTS

Why is Hiram Johnson still alive?—Because he's too mean to die!

—a popular maxim about California's four-term governor

Hiram [Johnson] always despised the only two things he didn't have—money and a sound mind.

—California saying

I was ashamed of being a Republican and afraid of being a Democrat.

—Robert W. Kenny, California politician

He has a mind like a miller bug—it just skates on the surface.

—Robert W. Kenny, about a colleague

Heard the wonderful news? [Franklin D.] Roosevelt died, and Bill Langer got killed going to the funeral.

—local story about Senator Bill Langer of North Dakota

We know Old Abe does not look very handsome, but if all the ugly men in the U.S. vote for him, he will surely be elected.

—Republican campaign propaganda, 1860

There are three sexes—men, women, and clergymen.

—Sydney Smith, clergyman, wit, and essayist

I have to believe in the Apostolic Succession. There is no other way of explaining the descent of the Bishop of Exeter from Judas Iscariot.

—Sydney Smith

The Puritans hated bear-baiting, not because it gave pain to the bear, but because it gave pleasure to the spectators.

—T.B. Macaulay, historian, essayist, poet, and statesman

She was brought up to work hard and she did. She was told "You make your bed and you lie in it," and she did, even if she lay in it alone.

—Ellen Goodman, columnist, on Pat Nixon, wife of U.S. president Richard Nixon

We have a petticoat Government! Mrs. Wilson [wife of U.S. President Woodrow Wilson] is President!

—Albert Fall, U.S. senator, during period of President Woodrow Wilson's illness when his wife assumed presidential duties

POLITICS AND POLITICIANS

In politics there is no honor.

—Benjamin Disraeli, British prime minister

Politicians are the same all over. They promise to build a bridge even where there is no river.

—Nikita Khrushchev, Soviet Communist leader

I am not a politician, and my other habits are good.

—Artemus Ward, writer

Politicians as a class radiate a powerful odor. Their business is almost as firmly grounded on false pretenses as that of the quack doctor or the shyster lawyer.

—H.L. Mencken, writer, editor, and critic

In statesmanship get the formalities right; never mind about the moralities.

—Mark Twain, writer and humorist

An ambassador is an honest man sent to lie abroad for his country.

—Sir Henry Wotton, poet and diplomat

The statesman shears the sheep, the politician skins them.

—Austin O'Malley, oculist

What have you done? cried Christine,
You've wrecked the whole party machine.
To lie in the nude may be rude,
But to lie in the House is obscene.

—Anonymous doggerel during Profumo scandal

I don't make jokes; I just watch the government and report the facts.

—Will Rogers, humorist and actor

Whenever a man has cast a longing eye on offices, a rottenness begins in his conduct.

—Thomas Jefferson, third U.S. president

POLITICAL PARTIES AND IDEOLOGIES

Democracy is also a form of religion; it is the worship of jackals by jackasses.

—H.L. Mencken, writer,
editor, and critic

If the Republicans stop telling lies about us, we will stop telling the truth about them.

—Adlai Stevenson, statesman

I never said all Democrats were saloonkeepers; what I said was all saloonkeepers were Democrats.

—Horace Greeley, journalist
and politician

[The 1960 Democratic Party Convention is] a cigar-smoking, stale-aired, slack-jawed, butt-littered, foul, bleak, hard-working, bureaucratic death gas of language and faces . . . lawyers, judges, ward heelers, mafiosos, Southern goons and grandees, grand old ladies, trade unionists and finks; [full] of pompous words and long pauses which lie like a leaden pain over fever.

—Norman Mailer, author

POLITICAL REFORMERS AND CORRUPTERS

Power corrupts. You use it, abuse it, then lose it.

—Henry Kaiser, industrialist

A reformer is a guy who rides through a sewer in a glass-bottomed boat.

—James J. Walker, mayor
of New York City

Four more years of those crack-pots and we are done—all finished—Eleanor and Sidney will take over and may the good Lord help us!

—from Texas campaign literature in
1944 opposing F.D. Roosevelt,
U.S. president

They are a lying, perjured, rum-soaked, and libidinous lot.

—Charles H. Parkhurst on Tammany Hall

The country is being run by a group of college professors. This Brain Trust is endeavoring to force socialism upon the American people.

—Henry D. Hatfield, U.S. senator

A conservative is man with two perfectly good legs, who, however, has never learned to walk.

—Franklin D. Roosevelt, U.S. president

A reactionary is a somnambulist walking backward.

—Anonymous

When I came into power, I found that the party managers had taken it all to themselves. I could not name my own Cabinet. They had sold out every place to pay the election expenses.

—Benjamin Harrison, U.S. president

You don't win campaigns with a diet of dishwater and mild toast.

—Richard M. Nixon, U.S president

ON THE PRESIDENCY

Why in hell does anybody want to be a head of state? Damned if I know.

—Harry S Truman, U.S. president

Being a President is like riding a tiger. A man has to keep on riding or be swallowed. The fantastically crowded months of 1945 taught me that a President either is constantly on top of events, or, if he hesitates, events will soon be on top of him. I never felt that I could let up for a moment.

—Harry S Truman

Truman: Why don't you run for governor, Bob?
Kenny: I don't have to run for office. I want to run away from it.
Truman: I've been doing that all my life, Bob, and look where I am now.
Kenny: Yes, and what you have now is a job without a future.

—a colloquy between President Truman
and Californian Robert W. Kenny
in July 1945

The first advice I am going to give my successor is to watch the generals and to avoid feeling that just because they were military men their opinions on military matters were worth a damn.

—John F. Kennedy, U.S. president

Jesus Christ, you guys are something else. When I was elected, you all said that my old man would run the country in consultation with the pope. Now here's the only thing he's ever asked me to do for him, and you guys piss all over me.

—John F. Kennedy, upon trying to appoint Francis Xavier Morrisey, his father's friend, to the Federal bench

When we got into office, the thing that surprised me most was that things were just as bad as we'd been saying they were.

—John F. Kennedy

My God! What is there in this place [Washington] that a man should ever want to get into it?

—James Abram Garfield, U.S. president

As to the Presidency, the two happiest days of my life were those of my entrance upon the office and my surrender of it.

—Martin Van Buren, U.S. president

My God, this is a hell of a job! I have no trouble with my enemies. But my damn friends, they're the ones that keep me walking the floor nights.

—Warren G. Harding, U.S. president

THE MEDIA

I always said that when we don't have to go through you bastards [journalists], we can really get our story over to the American people.

—John F. Kennedy, U.S. president, to correspondent Benjamin C. Bradlee, after a successful live television program (in 1962) in which correspondents asked direct questions

. . . an obese, malevolent fishwife, screaming journalistic obscenities at more than two million persons a day, exhorting them to go out and kill a commie for Christ—or even just for fun.

—James Aronson, editor, attacking
the New York *Daily News*

I act as a sponge. I soak it up and squeeze it out in ink every two weeks.

—Janet Flanner, on her
writing assignments

The news is the one thing networks can point to with pride. Everything else they do is crap, and they know it.

—Fred Friendly, former
CBS News president

QUIET LIVING

I am rather inclined to silence, and whether that be wise or not it is at least more unusual now-a-days to find a man who can hold his tongue than to find one who cannot.

—Abraham Lincoln, U.S. president

If you don't say anything, you won't be called on to repeat it.

—Calvin Coolidge, U.S. president

O that the desert were my dwelling place!

—Lord Byron in *Childe Harold*

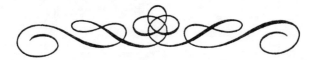

RACE RELATIONS

The economic situation of the Negroes in America is pathological.

—Gunnar Myrdal, Swedish economist
and sociologist

Harlem has a black belt where darkies dwell in a heaven and where white men seek a little hell.

—Alfred Kreymborg

Never trust a man whose eyes are too close to his nose.

—Lyndon B. Johnson, U.S. president

It is not good to be a Negro in the land of the free and the home of the brave.

—Rudyard Kipling, poet

The haughty American nation . . . makes the Negro clean its boots and then proves the . . . inferiority of the Negro by the fact that he is a bootblack.

—George Bernard Shaw, author
and critic

Me good Indian.

—Commanche Chief Toch-a-way

The only good Indian is a dead Indian.

—General Philip Sheridan

Segregation is not humiliating but a benefit, and ought to be so regarded by you gentlemen.

—Woodrow Wilson, U.S. president, in
a speech to black leaders in 1913

All I ask for the Negro is that if you do not like him, let him alone.

—Abraham Lincoln, U.S. president

As a nation, we began by declaring that "all men are created equal." We now practically read it, "All men are created equal, except Negroes." When the know-Nothings get control, it will read, "all men are created equal, except Negroes, and foreigners, and Catholics." When it comes to this I should prefer emigrating to some other country where they make no pretense of loving liberty—to Russia, for instance, where despotism can be taken pure, without the base alloy of hypocrisy.

—Abraham Lincoln

You and we are different races. We have between us a broader difference than exists between almost any other two races. Even when you cease to be slaves, you are yet far removed from being placed on an equality with the white race. You are cut off from many of the advantages which the other race enjoys. It is better for us both to be separated.

—Abraham Lincoln, during a meeting
with free Negro leaders, at the
White House, August 1862

RELIGIOUS CONCERNS

There has never been any more religion or decency in his sermons, or his exhortations, or his talk at death beds, than in the yelling of hyenas, the cursing of pirates, or the objurgations of harlots ... Heaven, earth, and even Hell, abhor him—though the latter will somehow manage to gulp him down.

> —George D. Prentice, Kentucky editor,
> evaluating William G. Brownlow, a
> local preacher and governor of
> Tennessee in the 1860s

The Pilgrim Fathers fell first on their knees and then on the aborigines.

> —Popular saying

ON SPORTS AND RECREATION

[Football is] one of the most dehumanizing experiences a person can face.

> —David Meggesi, voluntary retiree
> from professional football.

After losing another one in a pre-season game in Mexico:
Journalist: Did the altitude affect the Mets game?
Stengel: No, my players can lose at any altitude . . . The altitude always bothers my players even at Polo Grounds, which is below sea-level.

> —Casey Stengel, baseball manager

[The New York Yankees are] bleak perfectionists, insolent in their confidence, the snobs of the diamond. The Yankees are all technique, no color or juice.

> —Tallulah Bankhead, actress and
> New York Giants fan

I will not permit 30 men to travel 400 miles to agitate a bag of wind.

> —President White of Cornell University,
> expressing opposition to the estab-
> lishment of a football team

WRITERS AND WRITING

If a writer has to rob his mother, he will not hesitate; the "Ode on a Grecian Urn" is worth any number of old ladies.

—William Faulkner, novelist

How these authors magnify their office! One dishonest plumber does more harm that a hundred poetasters.

—Augustine Birrell, British essayist

I'm a Hollywood writer; so I put on a sports jacket and take off my brain.

—Ben Hecht, author

Satire lies about literary men while they live, and eulogy lies about them when they die.

—Voltaire, author and philosopher

I never saw such work or works. Campbell is lecturing— Moore idling—Southey twaddling—Wordsworth drivelling —Coleridge muddling—Joanna Baillie piddling—Bowles quibbling, squabbling, and snivelling.

—Lord Byron, poet

Let simple Wordsworth chime his childish verse,
And brother Coleridge lull the babe at nurse.

—Lord Byron

A pin has as much as some authors, and a good deal more point.

—G.D. Prentice, journalist

Get your facts first, and then you can distort 'em as you please.

—Mark Twain, novelist
and humorist

I took Eugene Sue's *Arthur* from the reading-room. It's indescribable, enough to make you vomit. You have to read this to realize the pitifulness of money, success and the public. Literature has become consumptive. It spits and slobbers, covers its blisters with salve and sticking-plaster, and has grown bald from too much hair-slicking. It would take Christs of art to cure this leper.

—Gustave Flaubert, author

This is not a novel to be tossed aside lightly. It should be thrown with great force.

—Dorothy Parker, short-story
and verse writer

Novels are receipts to make a whore.

—Matthew Green, poet

They lard their lean books with the fat of others' works.

—Robert Burton, scholar
and clergyman

Literature is the orchestration of platitudes

—Thornton Wilder, playwright
and novelist

Journalism is organized gossip.

—Edward Eggleston, author
and clergyman

The most truthful part of a newspaper is the advertisements.

—Thomas Jefferson, U.S president

Journalists write because they have nothing to say, and have something to say because they write.

—Karl Kraus, satirist